TRAINER'S MANUAL

Contact US!

Call center
English skills

Jane Lockwood
Hayley McCarthy

CAMBRIDGE
UNIVERSITY PRESS

CAMBRIDGE UNIVERSITY PRESS
Cambridge, New York, Melbourne, Madrid, Cape Town,
Singapore, São Paulo, Delhi, Tokyo, Mexico City

Cambridge University Press
79 Anson Road, #06-04/06, Singapore 079906

www.cambridge.org
Information on this title: www.cambridge.org/9780521178587

First published 2010
Reprinted 2011

Printed in Singapore by Markono Print Media Pte Ltd

ISBN 978-0-521-17858-7 paperback Trainer's Manual
ISBN 978-0-521-12473-7 paperback Coursebook colour edition with Audio CD

Additional resources for this publication at www.cambridge.org/elt/contactus

Authors' notes

Authoring credits

Steven Finch

Philippe Malin

Many thanks to both for their substantial contributions in writing sections of the coursebook, as well as their inspiration and support throughout the project.

Acknowledgments

Contact US! would not have been possible without the work and support of a number of colleagues and family members. First, we would like to acknowledge the company who worked on this project collaboratively: FuturePerfect. We would also like to thank the People2Outsource team, most particularly Vincent Bautista and Juan Miguel Brion, whose work piloting the course gave us invaluable insights into the call center trainer's experience of teaching these materials.

We would like to thank Neil Elias who provided early data for research into the nature of call center interaction. This coursebook would never have been possible without his support and advice on what the call center industry is really looking for in good customer communication. To Dan Elias, who inspired "Dan and Dora" and who tirelessly and patiently proofread, listened, and contributed.

Lastly, to all our friends and colleagues at Cambridge University Press. Thanks go out to the Hong Kong Cambridge University Press office for gallantly hosting so many working meetings and for their work on the *Contact US!* website. To Chris Boughton for his commitment to getting the coursebook started … and for the title! To Josep Mas as Publishing Manager, whose patience and attention to detail kept us all on track; and to Project Manager Chris Caridia, whose thoroughness and care have been essential to the success of this project.

Contents

*An extended downloadable pdf version of the Trainer's Manual,
with full step-by-step trainer's notes for each activity,
is available from http://www.cambridge.org/elt/contactus*

A trainer's guide to Contact US!

Contact US! has been designed for participants who already have a good level of proficiency (BUPLAS 3; CEF Low C1) and who want to "polish" their listening and speaking skills to attain a higher level of competency (BUPLAS 3.5; CEF High C1) before taking a customer services representative job in a call center. It aims to develop high-end professional English language communication skills when talking with American customers.

The 100-hour program is based around ten challenging authentic calls with customers. The customers represent a cross section of USA society in terms of ethnicity, age, geographic location, gender, and personality. The Customer Service Representatives (CSRs) in the calls represent a cross section of expert speaker and non-expert speaker models, and some of the calls are completed successfully, while others end unsuccessfully. The calls are taken across a range of industry types now being off-shored and outsourced to destinations such as India, the Philippines, Costa Rica, China, and Eastern Europe.

This program has been developed by the FuturePerfect Business English Specialists team, who are applied linguistic researchers, curriculum and materials designers, and assessment professionals specializing in the Business Process Outsourcing (BPO) industry, and call centers in particular. The team uses the outcomes of current exciting research to inform approaches to meeting the communication needs of non-expert speakers working in global call centers with practical teaching programs that really work and add impact. This program draws on the extensive experience of many leading global call centers and BPO organizations.

There are ten units in this level. Each unit contains ten hours of training material. The units have not been designed to be followed in a "lock–step" manner, and trainers are free to dip in and out of the book according to the needs of the group.

The frameworks

This coursebook is based on a sociolinguistic theoretical framework. This encompasses ways of exploring language and culture in context. The coursebook is aimed at adult learners and draws on best practice in adult learning. These frameworks are applied to communication development in the call center industry and exemplified in *Contact US!* Understanding these will help you to use the course to its full potential.

1. Linguistic frameworks

Contact US! is based on a sociolinguistic framework which emphasizes communicative effectiveness and interactive competence. A sociolinguistic framework (Halliday 1980) informs the analysis of authentic data for intercultural and linguistic breakdown, and further provides a framework for developing effective training material that addresses identified communicative needs. This framework encourages the trainer and student to consider the context in which communication takes place by identifying:

- **the audience** (who is talking to whom),
- **the purpose** (why the communication is taking place),
- **the content** (what is being communicated).

An understanding of the context will help the student make choices within the language system to make meaning.

Canale and Swain (1986) also provide a comprehensive and closely related communicative language teaching framework for language program development. Communicative competency includes:

- **linguistic competency** (range and accuracy of lexico-grammatical features),
- **discourse competency** (organization of the text),
- **phonological competency** (sound system including meanings made by word stress and intonation),
- **interactive competency** (building relationships in English),
- **strategic competency** (making repairs in English).

Each of these competency areas are systematically targeted in the different tasks and activities in *Contact US!* The frameworks ensure a well-rounded approach to call center communications training that will get results.

2. Adult learning frameworks

Contact US! is informed by professional development frameworks that recognize that adult learners go through clearly defined stages of learning (Dreyfus and Dreyfus 1986, Eraut 1994, Vygotsky). These frameworks provide the series with a principled approach to decisions about readiness for different kinds of training, and set realistic benchmarks for success.

Another adult learning framework relevant to this series is recognition of different learning styles and strategies (Willing 1988) within the group to ensure that learning is maximized and well targeted. Trainers need to be flexible with the individual students in their classes, and allow for different rates of and approaches to learning. Some will learn faster and some slower, while some will learn from a holistic approach and some from an analytical approach.

The other very important principle of adult learning that is embedded in **Contact US!** is a learner-centered approach to language learning. The role of the teacher is one of a facilitator. Much time is lost in teacher-centered training, where it is the trainer who talks rather than the trainee. Remember that every opportunity needs to be given to the learner/ trainees to use language in the classroom. For every minute of unnecessary time the trainer spends talking, the trainee is being "robbed" of valuable practice!

3. A communication assessment framework

Measuring communication outcomes as a result of communications training is a critical success factor for our industry clients. The series uses the Business Processing Language Assessment Scales (BUPLAS) developed by language specialists employed by FuturePerfect to measure communications gains.

Working again from a sociolinguistic model for language assessment, these scales and descriptors measure pronunciation, language and lexical accuracy and range, discourse competency, and interactive and strategic competency. Intercultural communication competencies are embedded in the discourse and interactive domains.

4. Intercultural framework

Language and culture are inextricably intertwined, as evidenced by the sociolinguistic approach described above.

Embedded in every call is rich cultural content. Therefore call centers require explicit cultural training. **Contact US!** uses the Early and Ang (2003) framework for conceptualizing components for intercultural training as follows:

- **Cognitive:** What knowledge do CSRs need regarding American culture, e.g., geographical, economical, historical, racial, etc?
- **Behavioral:** What behaviors are important to develop in the call center when communicating with American customers?
- **Motivational:** Motivating learners by demonstrating how culture impacts the success of call center transactions. In this course, behavioral and motivational factors are an integral part of the language and communication skills development program.

The specific intercultural tasks in the course deal with the cognitive aspect through input, then build on this to address the behavioral and motivational aspects through activities designed to develop intercultural communication skills. The input segments include:
- geographical information (maps, states, capital cities),
- regional differences that impact global communication,
- information related to the public and private domains of Americans,
- the USA as a multicultural society,
- American humor, sarcasm, and expectations of politeness and efficiency.

As a result of the sociolinguistic approach of the course, trainers and students will be encouraged to constantly consider the cultural dimensions of the authentic interaction in each of the units.

Tools and advice

1. Course delivery

To develop the students' performance as much as possible during the 100 hours of training, this course has been based on the principles of Communicative Language Teaching (CLT). In essence this approach aims to cut down "teacher talk time" and focus on students experiencing the practical application of language. The teacher is then in the role of facilitator: correcting and feeding back, while enabling situations in which students can practice productive and receptive language skills in an unrehearsed context.

About CLT

- Classroom goals are focused on all of the components of communicative competence and not restricted to grammatical or linguistic competence.

- Language techniques are designed to engage learners in the pragmatic, authentic, functional use of language for meaningful purposes. Organizational language forms are not the central focus, but rather aspects of language that enable the learner to accomplish those purposes.
- Fluency and accuracy are seen as complementary principles underlying communicative techniques. At times fluency may have to take on more importance than accuracy in order to keep learners meaningfully engaged in language use.
- In the communicative classroom, students ultimately have to use the language, productively and receptively, in unrehearsed contexts.

2. Providing correction and feedback

Correction and feedback are a fundamental function for every communication trainer in call center training or coaching. Without correction and feedback you will not be able to provide targeted individual help for your students, and the communicative language teaching approach will not be optimally applied.

The principles of correction and feedback

1. Correction relies on a good understanding of how language works in different forms of communication. Step one is making a good diagnosis of where the trainees' strengths and weaknesses lie from evidence they provide in the training, in the coaching, and on the floor. Do not rely on your own knowledge of L1 interference mistakes as these are often not the source of communication breakdown in a call center environment.
2. Feedback is one of the key requirements in successful learning. Both positive feedback and corrections must be given. Participants will benefit from knowing how well they are doing and what they still need to work on to reach the target level.
3. Those students who are less confident may need more positive feedback to encourage them.
4. More confident or advanced trainees will still need positive feedback—both positive feedback and corrections. In fact, some high level trainees may have "stabilized" errors, and they will need to have these errors brought to their attention in order to help them progress further in their accuracy skills.
5. Accuracy work will require more corrections and immediate feedback than fluency work, which also requires corrections and feedback, but not as immediately.
6. Some participants from certain cultures or with certain learning styles expect to be corrected by the trainer or praised when they are doing well in class; others may not welcome feedback as much, or might prefer to receive feedback in private. Clarifying expectations about feedback at the beginning of the course may help avoid tensions later.
7. Always give the participants the opportunity to correct themselves as some mistakes may simply be slips.
8. If a participant does not correct him/herself, give other participants an opportunity to correct a mistake. This is called peer evaluation. Not only will this help increase trainees' confidence if they are able to provide the correction, but involving other participants will help assess their level of understanding.

3. The syllabus

The purpose of this training is to prepare the students for dealing with customers in a call center environment. For this reason, the syllabus is based on current research findings into communication breakdown between customers and agents in call centers, as well as research into the key skills needed to be communicatively competent as a call center agent. While grammar and pronunciation are important, there are many other aspects of communication that your students will need to be confident in, and which are also covered in this course (such as extensive speaking and interpersonal communication).

Because the focus of the course is to enhance skills in dealing with customers in a call center, each unit is based on an authentic call. Students begin by listening to the call, and then go on to a series of language, communication, and intercultural exercises, all of which are relevant to the content of that specific call. When you are planning your syllabus, think about the following points:

- Feel free to delve into the coursebook wherever you like. It is not based on a progression of difficulty. All the units are challenging for students who are at a low C1 level (CEF) or BUPLAS 3.
- Do not feel disappointed if your students do not learn and apply everything you teach them in the language communication classroom. Some units will revisit language items for further practice. In this sense, you can view **Contact US!** as a spiral curriculum, circling back to the same skills through different contexts and approaches.

Introduction

Objectives and structure of a unit

Every student likes to know what to expect in their learning unit. Go through the unit objectives before you start it, and get agreement on the outcomes you expect. Some students at this early stage may want to articulate personal objectives for this unit of learning, e.g., "I want to be able to use English to actively listen to my customer."

Below is a detailed guide to each section of *Contact US!*

A The call (listening activities)

This section is divided as follows:

1. **Pre-listening exercise.** This is sometimes called "predictive" listening. Ask the students to think about and discuss in pairs what they think the call is going to be about? The title of the unit provides the clue. By doing this, the students invest something of themselves in the listening exercise. Thus, motivation is increased when it comes to listening to the call.

2. **Global listening activity.** When listening for the first time to a call, it is important to encourage the students not to try and understand everything that is said. At this early stage of the listening activity, it is important for the student to understand the "gist" of what is being discussed, i.e, a general understanding of the call (e.g., Is the customer angry?).

3. **Detailed listening activity.** After listening to the call and generally understanding what the purpose of the call is and who is talking to whom, it is then time to move onto the detail of the call. Detailed listening activities can include some or all of the following: information extraction, inference, interpreting, analyzing, and synthesizing.

Following is a more detailed guide for the *Contact US!* call center listening activities described above. Arouse the trainees' interest in the pre-listening activity by doing any of the following:

- Ask them to discuss answers to pre-listening questions.

- Relate what they are about to hear to their own lives or to something familiar to them (e.g., before listening to a customer support call, you can ask them to recall the times when they have had to call a company to seek customer support).

- Ask them to predict what might happen in the listening text.

- Give the participants some time (about a minute) to read the instructions and questions, especially if the listening task is a little complicated or there are comprehension questions to be answered while listening.

- Be sure to play the text loud enough for the participants to hear, especially when playing authentic material, which may be spoken fast. Don't be afraid to play the call again at any stage.

- For listening tasks that require the participants to listen for interpretative meaning, allow the trainees to discuss their answers before discussing them as a class in order to give everyone an opportunity to share their views. If views are very divergent, you can assign a reporter from each group to summarize the group's discussion.

B Focus on language

The language activities in each unit come directly out of the authentic call in that unit. The kinds of language-focus exercises that have been chosen relate to the frequency of that item in the call and/or where a grammatical item has caused communication breakdown. Contrary to what many people think, grammatical errors caused by first language interference do not, in general, cause communication breakdowns on the phone. Therefore, this course does not devote time to such errors. Instead, this section of each unit introduces and practices key areas of language that have been found to cause breakdown, either because they are used badly or because the agent does not have important language in his/her repertoire to make important meanings. For example, a customer who is very upset may require the agent to say something like "I really am terribly sorry about that; I wouldn't have sent it to that address if I'd known that!" as opposed to "I'm sorry I sent it to that address." The suggested flow of classroom activity for this section is as follows:

1. Present the language focus item to the group through the input box. Make sure you relate the language point to what occurred in the call. Grammar changes depending on the context, so, although trainees may "know" how the present progressive tense is formed in English, they may not know how it functions in specific contexts. As the call center transcript is central to this exercise, make sure students have the transcript when they are doing the exercise because they will be regularly asked to find examples of language in the transcript and deduce meaning.

2. As far as possible, get the trainees working in pairs or small groups to do the activities. This will provide them with an opportunity for discussion and an additional chance for them to practice their spoken language during the exercise.

3. Note that in this section the focus is on language accuracy. There are many controlled activities in this section. For some students this may be a little frustrating as they may be making mistakes that are "stabilized." These errors take a long time to eradicate, so the trainer needs to keep coming back to language focus revision throughout the course to check on the accuracy of these items.

4. Note also that in this section that the American idioms are regularly practiced, either because they appear in the call in the unit, or because they occur with high frequency in the existing corpus on call center interactions. Discussing the meaning of these expressions is important, but it will take time for the trainees to incorporate them into their language. And in some cases this may not be appropriate anyway. Distinguishing which ones should be understood only, as opposed to using them, is a useful exercise to do.

C Soft skills

The soft skills section of a unit relates directly to the call. In sociolinguistics, grammar is called functional grammar. This means it is grammar embedded in real situations, and it forms the basis of good soft skills. In each call an aspect of soft skills is targeted for practice. This may relate to the textual quality of the language (e.g., explaining things clearly), or it may relate to specific functional grammar items (e.g., "modality" in apologizing). For second language learning it is important to understand not only the intention of the soft skills, but also how this is expressed in English. A suggested guide for the activities is outlined below:

1. Relate the soft skills area clearly to the call. This may already have been done in the listening component, but introduce it again as the special focus of this section of the course.

2. Present the input. Trainers may want to add extra information from the web at this stage, but be careful not to make it too input-heavy. Always elicit experiences and ideas from the trainees to make this part of the lesson learner centered.

3. Relate the soft skills back to the call and elicit ideas on how well or poorly these may have been used. Not all the calls are model examples!

4. Ask the trainees to work in pairs when they apply their new soft skills. It is important to give the trainees time and support in what they are going to say. As they work in pairs, sitting back to back will provide a more challenging experience when they are interacting with each other.

5. Provide feedback to the trainees as you go around and listen. Depending on the level of confidence you may select one or two pairs to present their answers to the rest of the group and ask them for peer evaluations.

6. If you have recording equipment available, a valuable activity is to ask the pairs to record their exchange and then to play it back for self-evaluation. Sometimes trainees are regularly making mistakes they are not aware of!

D Pronunciation

As previously mentioned, pronunciation is important in building up good relationships with customers on the phone. However, this course does not attempt to develop an American accent, but instead aims at a more globally comprehensible accent that can be understood by other L1 and L2 speakers, who may call the call center for service. In each of the pronunciation exercises, different aspects will be practiced. Perhaps one of the most important aspects of using language in a call center is the use of word stress and intonation to convey meaning. Please note the suggested classroom activities below for this section of the course.

1. Explain to the class that pronunciation practice is a bit like losing weight or giving up smoking. It is a process that requires a high degree of self-motivation and a lot of practice to get results. These classroom exercises are just a "trigger," and trainees should try to spend at least one extra hour per day doing personal pronunciation exercises.

2. Often the section will start with a listening exercise. Research shows that if an L2 learner cannot recognize a certain sound in English, it will be difficult for him/her to reproduce it. The listening exercise may entail going back to the relevant bit in the call, or playing the whole recording again.

3. Ask the students to work in pairs for the production phase of the activities and provide peer and self-evaluation. The trainer should be circulating, listening closely, and providing feedback to pairs and individuals. Any common errors should be noted for full class feedback at the end of each activity.

4. The trainer may also like to note L2 phonological problems of specific groups of learners for special attention. However, the overall aim of pronunciation practice is not to sound American, but to be globally comprehensible.

Introduction

E Read and explain

This section of each unit is important because agents in call centers often have to read text from their screens, synthesize and analyze what they have read, and then give key bits of information to their customers. This is a very demanding skill and takes time to develop. The texts are largely taken from the business world, and there is an emphasis on describing procedures or providing information.

There is a time limit imposed on reading the texts, and trainers are advised to adhere to this as strictly as possible, as agents in the call centers work within very strict time limitations in such situations.

The paired exercise always asks the agent to explain clearly the relevant content from the text. This activity also provides an opportunity for the agent to demonstrate other aspects of good service such as soft skills, selection of appropriate language and vocabulary, and clarity and tone of voice. The suggested flow of classroom activities for this section of a unit are explained below:

- Ask the students to predict what kind of text they are going to read from the title and format of the text in front of them.
- Then ask the students to spend a minute skimming the reading text to get only a very general understanding.
- Move onto the paired activities which provide activities for the trainees to scan the text for details relevant to the caller's concerns. As you proceed through the course, tighten up the timings of each of these activities in line with the real situation in a call center. Agents need to be able to do this exercise in "real" time with accuracy and efficiency.
- Trainees may like to record their answers for self-evaluation. This extended activity will also provide extra practice if the students have found the activity difficult.

F Intercultural matters

The overall aim of this section is to highlight the similarities and differences between cultures as reflected in customer service during calls. The aim of the section is for trainees to understand that culture, too, is a negotiated process rather than a set of static facts to be learned. As outlined in the frameworks earlier in this guide, culture in **Contact US!** is presented accordingly, not just as a set of facts about a target locality and group of people, but also as a set of skills and attitudes to be negotiated. In order to avoid stereotyping Americans here, callers include varieties of Americans who are ethnically different and who represent a cross section of age, gender, personality, and socio-economic groups.

Each section builds on aspects of cultural knowledge, skills and attitudes that emerge from the call. Agents are encouraged to see intercultural relationship building in American call centers as a dynamic process involving both parties. In an ideal call, the agent will be able to make adjustments based on the tone and/or content of the customer's response to ensure that communication remains smooth.

A suggested classroom approach to intercultural matters is outlined as follows:

1. Relate the intercultural section to the initial call in terms of the theme and/or event. It is important that the trainees do not think that all Americans are alike, as this can result in unconstructive stereotyping and can create an unnecessary distance between the caller and the agent.
2. Provide the input. This can be extended by further relevant information downloaded from the web. However, be very prudent in your selections: make sure that the information comes from reputable websites and is backed up by at least two other reputable sources. Make sure that you don't turn this part of the course into a lecture on American culture. Be prepared to discuss this as you go along.
3. Move on quickly to relate this new cultural information to the trainees' own culture(s). Ask the students to work in pairs and groups to complete the activities. Discuss the outcomes at the end. Students may like to elect a reporter for this purpose. Make sure the groups/pairs know this before they start their discussions.
4. Relate the new information and discussion outcomes to how this may affect good service on the phones. For example, how to use language in an insurance claims call center to offer condolences to an older caller who has just lost a loved one.
5. Make links between this section of the course and other sections. Make students aware that the cultural sensitivity they have learned will be required in the final role-play activity.

G Role-play

The role-play brings everything together as a final activity in each unit. Make it clear to the trainees that this is a fluency activity, where you expect them to take risks and speak extensively. The following procedure is a guide for trainers for this final activity:

1. You may want to revise some of the language focus and soft skills language before you start, as each role-play relates to the soft skills area in the unit.

2. Read through the scenario as a class and make sure students understand it fully. Trainers are free to add extra complexity if they wish.

3. Split the class into pairs and get the trainees sitting back to back if possible. In this way they can simulate being on the phone where they can't see the facial expressions of the person they are talking to. This makes the role-play more authentic.

4. Give each member of the pair either Rolecard 1 or Rolecard 2 to read. Make sure they understand their role. You may want trainees with the same rolecards to sit together and prepare their roles.

5. Put a time limit on the role-play. Normally each role-play should be resolved in about five minutes. Average handling time (AHT) and first time resolution (FTR) are very significant issues in call centers to the point where long rambling calls with no outcome have become a business problem. An agent's performance is measured against these criteria, as well as others such as communication skills. For this reason, it is important that your students practice putting their skills into action in a reasonable time limit.

6. Make sure you go around monitoring the groups, noting down the strengths and weaknesses for feedback at the end of the role-play activity.

7. When the role-play is finished, ensure that you allow a debrief time where the trainees are able to tell the rest of the group how they think they did. This is important. Depending on the confidence levels of the groups, you may invite one or two pairs to come forward and do their role-play for the rest of the group for peer evaluation purposes. Your debrief should not pick up on every mistake the trainees have made, but should focus more on those areas of communication that you felt threatened communication, or where improvement was obviously required.

8. After the debrief and/or peer evaluation activity, provide the students with your feedback on how they performed. Here the focus should be on language and phonological strengths and weaknesses, intercultural sensitivity, soft skills handling, and listening capability.

H Self-evaluation

This section of each unit gives the trainee the chance to review his/her performance throughout the unit. It is a time for the trainee to make renewed commitment to those parts of the program where he/she needs to do extra practice.

Ask the trainees to complete this part out of class, but allocate time within the class for trainees to share their personal reflections. This may lead to informal networks of trainees working together on common areas of need. If the self-evaluation is done just prior to going on to the floor or even as part of a coaching solution, the self-diagnostic aspect of this section will save valuable time on the part of the coach and lead to quicker communication support solutions.

Sources

Canale, M., Swain, M. (1980) 'Theoretical bases of communicative approaches to second language teaching and testing', *Applied Linguistics* 1, 1-47.

Dreyfus, H., Dreyfus, S. (1986) *Mind Over Machine,* USA: The Free Press.

Eraut, M. (1994) *Developing Professional Knowledge and Competence,* UK: The Falmer Press.

Halliday, M.A.K (1985) *An Introduction to Functional Grammar,* London: Arnold.

Willing, K. (1988) *Learning Styles in Adult Migrant Education,* Australia: NCRC.

A The call

The caller has phoned the Atlantic Aroma Coffee Center because she is interested in acquiring a coffee shop franchise. She retired from her previous business and now has a coffee shop, which she would like to brand Atlantic. She is exploring this idea of the franchise for the first time and needs some information. The agent asks her a number of questions, sends her a form to fill out, and explains that a rep will contact her.

1 Pre-listening activity

Answer key (suggested)

It is possible that the call could be about opening a franchise of a company. By saying "I've always wanted to," the caller is implying that this is a dream that she has had for a long time.

2 Global listening activity

Answer key

1. Rajiv, Customer Service Agent for Atlantic Aroma Coffee Center and a caller, Ashley Green, who is interested in an Atlantic coffee shop franchise.

2. The caller is inquiring about what she needs to do to acquire an Atlantic Aroma coffee shop franchise.

3 Detailed listening activity

Answer key

1. F	5. T
2. F	6. T
3. F	7. T
4. T	8. T

B Focus on language

1 Forming questions in spoken English

1

Answer key

Full grammatical question form
And do you just want to brand it Atlantic?
OK, do you want to do that?
What is your first name?
What is your phone number?
Did you receive/get it?

2 Open and closed questions

1

Answer key (suggested)

Agent: Good evening. This is Ken, how may I help you?

Caller: Yes, I've lost my credit card and maybe someone has stolen it. I was out shopping and I used it yesterday, but …

Agent: OK, let me take a few details and I'll do my best to help you. Can I take your name and Social Security number?

Caller: Yes, my name is Martha Lewis and my Social Security is 378 59 2300.

Agent: And you think you've lost your card?

Caller: Well, it might have been stolen and that's what I'm afraid of …

Agent: Have you tried looking for it?

Caller: Yes, I've just been looking in the normal places. You know – bedroom, under the bed. That's where I always keep my money, you know.

Agent: When do you last remember using it, ma'am?

Caller: Just a couple of days ago when I went to the supermarket. I spent about $125 on groceries.

Agent: Have you checked that the supermarket doesn't have your card, ma'am?

Caller: Oh, I hadn't thought about that. Perhaps I should go back and check there.

Agent: I think that would be a good idea. Is it possible that you left it somewhere else?

Caller: Oh, you never know, and last night I went out with a couple of friends and my bag zipper was open when I left the bar. It was a bit strange, but I didn't think anything was stolen. But now I'm worried, I think I should report it stolen, just in case. You know, be on the safe side.

Agent: Yes, I understand your concern. Would you like us to cancel the card, ma'am?

Caller: No, I'll go back to the supermarket and if it's not there, I'll give you another call.

Agent: Would you like me to put a temporary hold/stop on your card?

Caller: OK, that sounds like a good idea. A temporary stop would be good. Just so no one can run up my credit!

Agent: May I have the credit card number, please?

Caller: 84692672057

Agent: And can I have your Social Security number again, ma'am?

Caller: Social Security is 378 59 2300.

Agent: And your date of birth, please?

Caller: April 10th, 1969.

Agent: OK, that's all done, it's on temporary hold. And give me a call tomorrow. I really hope you find it, Martha. Thank you for calling.

Caller: Thanks, bye.

2

Answer key (suggested)

Short-cut question form	Full grammatical question form
Name and Social Security number, please?	Can I take your name and Social Security number?
How about checking the supermarket?	Have you checked that the supermarket doesn't have your card, ma'am?

We should cancel the card?	Would you like us to cancel the card, ma'am?
Your card number, please?	May I have the credit card number, please?
And your Social Security number?	And can I have your Social Security number again, ma'am?

3 American idioms (1)

1

Answer key

1.	i	6.	c
2.	g	7.	b
3.	f	8.	h
4.	d	9.	a
5.	e		

2

Answer key (suggested)

Idiomatic expression	Meaning
head off	to leave
head in	go inside
have a good head on one's shoulders	to be sensible and/ or smart
head up	lead
head for	aim for/ walk toward
he's off his head	he's crazy
keep your head	keep calm
put our heads together	discuss our ideas

C Soft skills

2 Putting the customer on hold

Answer key (suggested)

Scenario 1

Customer: I get the impression you don't get my question.

Agent: I understand your question completely, sir/ma'am. However, I do not have that information available now. Is it all right with you if I put you on hold for a moment while I check with my supervisor? Together we will do our best to solve this issue for you.

Scenario 2

Customer: Now, look. We're not getting anywhere! I want to talk to your supervisor.

Agent: I'm very sorry this is causing so much frustration for you, and I understand that you would like to speak to a supervisor about it. Do you mind waiting for a minute or two while I check if a supervisor is available to talk to you right now?

D Pronunciation

1 Rising intonation: asking questions and opening up interaction

2

Answer key (suggested)

1. How can I assist you?
2. And you just want to brand it Atlantic?
3. And your first name?
4. Can I just put you on hold for a second?
5. Uhm, is that necessary?

2 Falling intonation: closing down an interaction

2

Answer key (suggested)

1. That's exactly right – the second.
2. Sure, no problem.
3. All right, that has been sent out to you.
4. Yes, in about a week, a rep will make contact.
5. You've been very helpful.

3 Syllable stress

1

Answer key

STATE	Number of syllables	Stressed syllable
Arkansas	3	AR·kan·**sas**
California	4	**cal**·i·FOR·nia
Connecticut	4	con·NECT·i·cut
Florida	3	FLOR·i·da
Georgia	2	GEOR·gia
Illinois	3	**il**·li·NOIS
Louisiana	5	lou·**I**·si·AN·a
Massachusetts	4	**mas**·sa·CHU·setts
Michigan	3	MICH·i·gan
Mississippi	4	**mis**·sis·SIP·pi
Missouri	3	mis·SOU·ri
New Jersey	3	new JER·sey
New York	2	new YORK
North Dakota	4	north da·KO·ta
Ohio	3	o·HI·o
Pennsylvania	4	**penn**·syl·VA·nia
Tennessee	3	**TEN**·nes·SEE
Texas	2	TEX·as
Virginia	3	vir·GIN·ia
Wisconsin	3	wis·CON·sin

4 Consonant clusters

1

Answer key

Florida – "fl"
Indiana – "nd"
North Dakota – "thd"
Pennsylvania – "ns," "lv"
Wisconsin – "sc," "ns"

NB: Connecticut – "ct": the c is not pronounced.

2

Answer key (suggested)

"Than**k y**ou for calli**ng** A**tl**antic Aroma Coffee Center. We are here to provide you e**xcell**e**nt** cu**st**omer service. My name is Rajiv. How can I assi**st** you?" "I'**m w**anting to find out about um in**f**ormation on a **franch**ise opportuni**ty**."

F Intercultural matters

1 Geography of the United States

2

→ See **Appendix 1**

The alphabetical order of states is:

1. Alabama	26. Montana
2. Alaska	27. Nebraska
3. Arizona	28. Nevada
4. Arkansas	29. New Hampshire
5. California	30. New Jersey
6. Colorado	31. New Mexico
7. Connecticut	32. New York
8. Delaware	33. North Carolina
9. Florida	34. North Dakota
10. Georgia	35. Ohio
11. Hawaii	36. Oklahoma
12. Idaho	37. Oregon
13. Illinois	38. Pennsylvania
14. Indiana	39. Rhode Island
15. Iowa	40. South Carolina
16. Kansas	41. South Dakota
17. Kentucky	42. Tennessee
18. Louisiana	43. Texas
19. Maine	44. Utah
20. Maryland	45. Vermont
21. Massachusetts	46. Virginia
22. Michigan	47. Washington
23. Minnesota	48. West Virginia
24. Mississippi	49. Wisconsin
25. Missouri	50. Wyoming

2 Retirement in the United States

4

Answer key *(suggested)*

Description of the caller:

- Proactive – caller asks if there is a website the agent can direct her to and asks a lot of questions about the process and what she needs to do throughout the call.

- Polite – caller says, "Sure, no problem" to being put on hold; maintains polite and friendly intonation throughout the call and thanks agent for being "very helpful."

- Friendly – caller jokes with agent that she left her business because she "got sick of all the lunches with the girls … you know." By sharing personal information in a humorous manner, the caller is building rapport with the agent.

Attitude toward retirement:

The caller has retired from business partly because of "all the lunches with the girls." This probably refers to her dislike of the expectation for her to have regular working lunches for business/networking purposes. The content of the call indicates that she sees her retirement as an opportunity to do something she really wants to do – run her own franchise.

G Role-play

Specifically, learners should practice:

- listening to understand the purpose of the call and the feelings of the caller ❑ **agent**
- using question forms correctly and appropriately to help interaction ❑ **agent**
- using American idioms appropriately ❑ **agent and caller**
- explaining information in a linear and logical manner ❑ **agent**
- giving information and asking questions for further clarification ❑ **caller**
- putting the customer on hold ❑ **agent**
- using intonation to open up and close down an interaction ❑ **agent and caller**
- using correct syllable stress (particularly for pronouncing state names) ❑ **agent and caller**
- pronouncing consonant clusters correctly ❑ **agent and caller**
- using intercultural knowledge *(geographical)* to help the conversation ❑ **agent**

H Self-evaluation

Direct learners to evaluate themselves in particular with regard to:

- how confident they are listening to understand the purpose and the feelings of the caller,
- using language to ask questions and make appropriate responses,
- their ability to give clear, concise explanations,
- using intonation to ensure comprehensibility and to ask questions in an appropriate manner,
- reading a text and synthesizing information to answer a caller's enquiry awareness of U.S. geography and U.S. attitudes to work and retirement.

2 Predicting customer need

A The call

The caller wants to buy medicine for his cattle as a bulk order. His cattle are dying and the need for a bulk order is a cost-cutting and time-saving solution that the vet had advised. The agent informs the customer that this is not allowed under company policy, and is generally unsympathetic to the customer's obvious concern and frustration.

1 Pre-listening activity

> **Answer key (suggested)**
>
> *Mess around with something* is an idiomatic expression meaning to waste time or effort. "I don't want to mess around with small amounts" suggests that the caller wants to buy a large amount of something, which could mean that this call will be about the quantity of an order.

2 Global listening activity

> **Answer key**
>
> Sentence 2.

3 Detailed listening activity

> **Answer key**
>
> 1. Denver, Colorado.
> 2. The caller's cows are dying so he wants to buy a bulk order of Colixin from a nearby store.
> 3. Main outlets on the stock list.
> 4. No. All sales must go through the company's distributors.
> 5. The caller is feeling frustrated and dissatisfied, and decides to order from another company.
> 6. Average to poor. The agent shows no sympathy for the caller's problem (dying cows) and is not proactive in finding an alternative solution.
>
> Suggested extra questions:
>
> 7. Does the agent sound confident when dealing with the caller's query?
> 8. Why are the caller's cows dying?

B Focus on language

1 Present continuous (1)

1

> **Answer key**
>
> The present continuous used for actions in progress:
>> I'm ringing up from …
>> I'm just inquiring …
>> (The cattle) are coming down with colic.
>> They're dying from it.
>> I'm trying to find out …
>> What's happening …
>> They're eating and chewing up dirt.
>> This is what we're going through.
>> The vets are telling us to use …
>
> The present continuous used to refer to the future:
>> We're going to use one cup a week …
>> We're going to use it on all of them.

2

> **Answer key**
>
> 2. love
> 3. don't understand
> 4. is talking
> 5. know
> 6. think

2 Using *just*

1

> **Answer key**
>
> 2. S   3. C   4. S   5. S

2

> **Answer key (suggested)**
>
> 1. We've **just** sent it to you this morning. / Let me **just** check that it has been sent.
> 2. It's very simple. It'll **just** take a few moments to explain. / OK, first of all, **just** press 234 then …

3. I **just** needed to make sure we had the right information. I'm sorry for the delay. / If you could **just** bear with us, sir, I'll be **just** a few more minutes.

4. Certainly, let me **just** transfer you. / Of course, would you mind holding for **just** a moment please while I transfer you?

3 Phrasal verbs (1)

1

Answer key

1. comes across
2. come over
3. come down with
4. came up with
5. came into

2

Answer key *(suggested)*

coming down with (l. 6)
find out (l. 12)
going through (l. 23)
go for it (l. 53)
pick up (l. 58)
mess around with (l. 94)

C Soft skills

1 Predicting caller need

1

Answer key *(suggested)*

Yes, I see what you're saying. You need a very large amount of this product because of the size of your herd and the costs involved. I'm not entirely sure if we can get it to you in bulk, but let me go and find out for you now. Do you mind waiting, or would you like us to call back?

2

Answer key *(suggested)*

1.

Caller means: I'm really concerned about missing my flight. What can you do to help me out?

Your response: Oh no! That must be very stressful for you. Don't worry. I'm going to do my best to make sure you get on a flight safe and sound. Let me go ahead and check on the status of your flight and find out when the next flight to New York is.

2.

Caller means: My phone no longer works. I need a replacement.

Your response: Oh dear, what a shame! We may be able to repair this phone if you send it back to us. I can also email you a brochure of new phones so you can see what is available in case repair isn't possible.

3.

Caller means: I think I've lost all the work that I just finished. Is there a way to get it back so I don't have to start all over?

Your response: I'm very sorry to hear that. You may be able to get your data back through the automatic system recovery program. I can guide you through the process.

4.

Caller means: I never use my credit card, and it's more of a pain than a convenience. I want to cancel it.

Your response: If you'd like to cancel your card, we can organize that for you. However, putting a stop to this card and ordering a new one is a simple process and won't take more than a couple of minutes. You'll receive your new card within three working days. Also, if you're concerned about losing it in the future, you may want to consider using our online banking function. I can guide you through how to use that if you are interested.

5.

Caller means: I need a birthday gift related to gardening as soon as possible.

Your response: We have plenty of gardening-related books in stock which we can get to Alaska in the next couple of days. Do you think your grandmother would appreciate a new gardening book?

2 Backchanneling

2

Answer key (suggested)

Unit 1
Agent [Caller]: A-S-H dot 34 at yahoo.com.
[That's correct.]

Agent [Caller]: 273 [uh-huh] Rockport Ave [Uh-huh] Sheldon [S-H-E-L-D-O-N?] Exactly.
[All right.] Missouri, MO [Mmm-hmmm.] 65109
[Thank you.] No, I'm sorry. Let me redo the zip code: 65020.

Unit 2
[Agent] Caller: I'm just ringing up from Denver …
[Colorado?]

Caller: … This is what we're going through.
Agent: OK.
Caller: Yes, and the vets are telling us to use Colixin powder.
Agent: OK.

3

Answer key (suggested)

Were there any differences in terms of backchanneling?
Yes, in Unit 1 the agent is more confident about backchanneling during extended speech.
In Unit 2 the agent uses backchanneling to react, often with confusion, when the caller stops speaking rather than showing continuous acknowledgment and understanding. She uses "OK" frequently when a fuller response might be expected, or when she might signal more clearly that she understands, or when she might request further clarification if she doesn't.
In the end she loses control of the call.

Were there differences in the way the calls ended?
In Unit 1 the call ended successfully with the caller having achieved the purpose of her call in a relatively short space of time. She says to the agent: "You've been very helpful." In Unit 2 the call ends with the caller expressing frustration at the company not being able to accommodate his particular needs ("That's crazy.") and stating his intention to take his business elsewhere.

Which caller is happier?
The caller in Unit 1 (see previous answer).

Which call is better for business?
Unit 1 is better for business because the caller's positive experience might encourage her to open a franchise. In Unit 2 the company has lost a customer. Although there are some things that will always be not allowed by company policy, this agent did not show a good, sympathetic understanding of the situation, and therefore could not build a good customer relationship that might encourage the customer to use Pet Fix again in the future.

4

Answer key (suggested)

1. [Oh it's still misspelled, I'm sorry about that …]
2. Good morning. [Good morning.] I'm inquiring about the application process for an auto loan. [Uh-huh, sure.]
3. Hi there. [Hello] I'm a little confused with this application form. [Right …] Can you guide me through it? [Sure, happy to.]
4. Yeah, I'm calling about my latest invoice. [Uh-huh] How did you come up with it? I'm not paying this! [Your last invoice, you say … OK …]
5. Connect to your supervisor right away! [A supervisor … let me see if she's available]

D Pronunciation

1 Contractions

1

Answer key

'm l. 3 I'm (ringing up …), l. 4 I'm (just inquiring …), l. 12 I'm (trying to find out), l. 63 I'm (not paying …), l. 86 I'm (sorry, but …)

've l. 5 I've (got a herd …), l. 22 we've (had a couple …), l. 30 we've (got …), l. 107 I've (already consulted …)

're l. 7 they're (dying from it …), l. 20 they're (eating …), l. 28 We're (going to …)

's l. 16 It's (for the cattle …), l. 18 What's (happening is …), l. 19 there's (uh no grass …), l. 51 here's (the …), l. 57 that's (no good …), l. 93 That's (what the vet said …), l. 96 it's (a company policy …), l. 100 That's (ridiculous …), l. 118 that's (crazy …)

'll l. 34 I'll (just check some …), l. 45 I'll (give you …), l. 48 you'll (need to …), l. 55 I'll (just give you …), l. 104 I'll (ask my supervisor …), l. 118 we'll (go to another company.)

n't l. 57 I can't (travel …), l. 59 I can't (leave …), l. 66 we don't (have information …), l. 74 they don't (do bulk, …), l. 75 don't you (package it …) l. 75 isn't it …? l. 76 aren't … aren't I (in the place …), l. 86 we really don't (um do that …), l. 109 we don't (have any …), l. 114 we really don't (um directly sell …)

3

Answer key

1. a) It is closed or it has closed (recently). Perhaps it will open again. (Possible scenario: standing outside a closed shop door.)
    b) It closed sometime in the past, perhaps forever.
2. a) We are married now at the moment of speaking. A long-standing situation.
    b) An action in the past, i.e., we got married.
3. a) He started playing long ago and is still playing at the moment of speaking. (he's = he has)
    b) This refers to the past only. It suggests he no longer plays musical instruments.
4. a) An invitation to have tea together in the future.
    b) A general enjoyment of having tea together. (Also: "I like having tea with you.")

2 /s/ or /z/

1

Answer key (suggested)

m   What room's his? /z/
l   That mall's got everything. /z/
th   Beth's taking a vacation. /s/
e   There's still time. /z/
f   The leaf's green. /s/
r   I see your father's got a new car. /z/
a   The area's too small. /z/

2

Answer key

l. 16   it's (for the cattle …) = it is
l. 18   What's (happening is …) = What is
l. 19   there's (uh no grass …) = there is /z/
l. 51   here's (the …) = here is /z/
l. 57   that's (no good …) = that is
l. 93   That's (what the vet said …) = that is
l. 96   It's (a company policy …) = it is
l. 100   That's (ridiculous …) = That is
l. 118   that's (crazy …) = that is

F Intercultural matters

1 American farming and ranch culture

2

Answer key (suggested)

1. lower than average level of education
2. lower than average income – insecure income because of unpredictable factors
3. probably from one of the dominant farming states
4. center-right (Republican) political views
5. Christian (possibly Baptist)
6. family and community oriented
7. rural environment often far from social centers and commercial conveniences

3

Customer profile	Agent service skills
Lower than average education levels	Be careful to simplify potentially complex language and content.
Environmental impact is important	Be sympathetic to environmental problems (such as disease, poor weather) because this directly impacts the income of the whole family.
Far away from big cities	Be proactive in finding solutions that will be more practical for the customer (e.g., home delivery rather than store pick-up).

2 Customer expectations: "thinking outside the box"

1

> **Answer key**
>
> Examples of the customer asking for individualized service are:
>
> 1. l. 31–32 "I wonder if we can get it in bulk. And how big? And how much?"
> 2. l. 61–64 "… Can I speak to the managing director about getting a bulk order because we need 60, 80, about 100 pounds of that stuff, and I'm not paying for 20-ounce jars."
> 3. l. 82–85 "I want to buy a real big box of this stuff … you know, you know – loose … that we actually get in pounds for these cattle."
> 4. l. 89–90 "Can I speak to your supervisor then? Please, because you must be able to get it straight from the factory before they package it up and get it from there and put it in a big bag or a big box."
>
> Agent responses in each case are:
>
> 1. l. 40–42 Agent doesn't answer the caller's question. After putting the caller on hold, the agent says: "… you can only buy the Colixin product from our main outlets on the stock list." Agent does not address whether the caller can buy in bulk, how big the bulk can be, or how much it will cost.
> 2. l. 65–70 Agent ignores the caller's request to speak to the managing director, and says that they do not have information about bulk purchases.
> 3. l. 86–88 Agent responds by apologizing and saying that this is not possible: "I'm sorry, but we don't do that; we don't have any larger sizes here."
> 4. l. 96–97 Agent does not transfer the caller to the supervisor, but says, "But we don't do that actually; it's a company policy." Agent does not suggest any alternative options to the caller or express sympathy for his predicament.
>
> Discussion questions:
>
> 1. The agent did not do a very good job. The agent did not quickly grasp what was going on (she gave stock list information rather than answering the caller's questions about the quantities and costs involved in bulk buying). She responded with robotic, mechanical-sounding answers about the outlets, and did not think outside the box or engage actively with the customer's predicament. The agent was not sympathetic to the problem, and did not appear to understand how important and urgent this was to the customer.
> 2. The agent did not seem to understand that the customer wanted individualized service. The agent appeared perplexed by the request to do something that the company "does not do." The customer was aware that this was an unusual request but wanted the company to provide special individualized service because of the circumstances. The agent just reiterated "but we don't do that" and "it's a company policy." If the agent had understood that the customer wanted individualized service, she could have tried to find out if it was possible (under the circumstances). If it was not possible she could have replied: "I'm sorry, we'd like to be able to help out in this terrible situation, but we aren't authorized to sell in bulk to private consumers."
> 3. The agent did not think outside the box at all. The agent was not proactive in offering solutions that could help the customer, considering that he cannot travel far from his sick cattle and needs to buy large quantities of medicine quickly. The agent offered unhelpful solutions (e.g., outlet names) and did not explore possibilities that would meet the customer's needs.

Answer key (suggested)

Customer profile	Agent service skills
Customer does not want to deal with store outlets, especially when they are far away. He wants to deal directly with the animal pharmaceutical company in order to bulk-buy and save costs.	Acknowledge that the customer wants something unusual (large quantities) and the reasons why. Be sympathetic to this request, rather than simply repeating that he should contact the store outlets. Offer to find out whether an exception can be made in this case.
Customer cannot travel far. He says: "I need somebody right here in Denver."	Engage with the customer's limitations (not being able to travel outside of Denver) and look for solutions that meet these needs.
Customer is cost-conscious: the problem is an extensive one and his main aim in buying in bulk is to save money. He wants to know the cost of buying in bulk and says that he's "not paying for 20-ounce jars."	Be sympathetic about how expensive medicine in this quantity will be, if bulk-buying is not an option, e.g., "Yes, I can see how it would be expensive to buy 100 pounds in 20-ounce containers … let me see whether we have a policy regarding bulk orders."

G Role-play

Specifically learners should practice:
- listening to understand the purpose of the call and the feelings of the caller ❑ **agent**
- using the present continuous correctly and appropriately ❑ **agent and caller**
- using *just* to emphasize or simplify ❑ **agent and caller**
- using phrasal verbs appropriately ❑ **agent and caller**
- predicting caller need ❑ **agent**
- backchanneling ❑ **agent**
- using contractions (including /s/ and /z/ endings) correctly ❑ **agent and caller**
- profiling customers for individualized service; thinking outside the box ❑ **agent**

H Self-evaluation

Learners should evaluate themselves in particular with regard to:
- how confident they are listening to understand the purpose and details of the call and the feelings of the caller,
- using the present continuous tense, phrasal verbs and *just*,
- their ability to predict customer needs and to backchannel,
- how confident they are using contracted forms,
- their ability to read a text and synthesize information to answer a caller's enquiry,
- using cultural information to profile a customer, thinking outside the box, and providing individualized customer service.

3 Explaining and giving instructions

A The call

The caller wants to change her phone number so that she can increase her privacy. She appears to find the process of changing her number tedious, indicated by her mostly monosyllabic responses. The agent is cheerful and helpful and is able to address the caller's needs.

1 Pre-listening activity

Answer key (suggested)

"I don't want people to have my phone details" suggests that the caller wants to limit the number of people who can contact him/her on his/her phone. The call may be about increasing the caller's phone privacy.

2 Global listening activity

Answer key (suggested)

Agent: confident, helpful, informative, efficient

Caller: preoccupied, bored

3 Detailed listening activity

Answer key

Tap the hash key twice.
Type in the number 1314.
Type in the number 33.
Type in another hash key.
Enter your new number.
Tap on the MS ID field.
Enter your old number.
Press the space dialog box.
Say something like "Congratulations."
Leave the phone for four hours.

B Focus on language

1 Zero conditional

Answer key (suggested)

1. *Or if you want to override that caller-ID block, you just press 428 and then the number, ok?*
How it is used: Communicates a **fact** and functions as an **instruction**.

2. *If you're in an elevator, you break up.*
How it is used: Communicates a general **fact** and functions as a **request** not to use the elevator during the conversation.

3. *If you want to put it on charger, then please do so, ok?*
How it is used: Communicates a **possibility**.

4. *You know if you go over, it cuts out the service, ok?*
How it is used: Communicates a general **fact** and functions as a **warning**.

2 Giving instructions using imperatives and softeners

2

Answer key (suggested)

l. 16   May I please have your cell phone number? (Not: Please give me …)
l. 26   May I have your name please? (Not: Give me, …)
l. 38   May I know why … (Not: Tell me …)
l. 66   Um, you might want to … write down your new number, OK?
l. 82   I want you to turn on your Quatro Fast Phone.
l. 90   I need you to tap the hash key twice.
l. 107   I want you to enter your new number there.
l. 112   I want you to tap on that line and enter your old Fast Phone cell phone number.
l. 122   I want you to press space, on the space dialog box.
l. 134   Now, you need to leave that phone …
l. 152   … I'd like to inform you …
l. 160   You could make some partial payments …

3 Using idioms

1

> **Answer key**
>
> | | |
> |---|---|
> | 1. c | 6. e |
> | 2. d | 7. i |
> | 3. j | 8. g |
> | 4. b | 9. h |
> | 5. a | 10. f |

2

→ See **Appendix 2**

> **Sample dialog**
>
> **A:** Good afternoon. May I help you?
>
> **B:** My sister is a vegetarian and you have delivered the wrong food basket to her.
>
> **A:** Could I please ask you **to take a look** at the basket for me and describe its contents?
>
> **B:** **It is down to you** to deliver the right basket at once. What are you going to do about that?
>
> **A:** I'm terribly sorry ma'am. Could you please give me your sister's address … and telephone number …
>
> **B:** This is a disgrace. I'm most dissatisfied.
>
> **A:** I'm terribly sorry about the confusion, ma'am.
> …………

C Soft skills

1 Giving clear instructions and explanations

1

> **Answer key** (suggested)
>
> 1. Keep the language simple. Don't use unnecessary jargon or idioms:
> l. 45 "You mean like a caller-ID doesn't appear with your number?"
>
> 2. Start with a summary statement:
> l. 77 "I'm gonna guide you through the programming steps."
>
> 3. Start each point with the main topic and then expand:
> l. 61 "… let me prepare your line to change the number, OK?"
>
> 4. Check understanding with the caller as you go along:
> l. 103 "And this'll highlight your number … right?"

5. Summarize at the end and check understanding:
l. 141. "Let me just give you a quick recap. I was able to change your number. Just remember your new number is 615-300-8358, OK?"

6. Remember … to modify your explanations and instructions for your audience:
l. 132 "Now leave that phone a bit for four hours for the programming to work."

D Pronunciation

1 Connected speech

1

> **Answer key**
>
> **Principle 1**   l. 18 "Han<u>g o</u>n, …"
> **Principle 2**   l. 15 "I'm gonna guide you t<u>o</u> activating …" /w/
>   l. 2 "How ma<u>y I</u> help you?" /j/
> **Principle 3**   l. 34 "Give me so<u>me m</u>ore time, OK?"

2

> **Answer key** (suggested)
>
> **Principle 1**
>
> 1. I don't belie<u>ve I</u> said for you to do that!
> 3. Can't you see it the<u>re in</u> the account details?
> 4. Thi<u>s is</u> simply unacceptable.
> 5. I thought tha<u>t I</u> was getting <u>a</u> full refun<u>d a</u> mon<u>th ago</u>? You'<u>ve a</u>lways said that I was.
>
> **Principle 2**
>
> 2. Wh<u>o a</u>sked for that to be done?
> 3. Can't you <u>see i</u>t there in th<u>e a</u>ccount details?
> 4. This is simpl<u>y u</u>nacceptable.
> 6. Never mind that now. Let me speak t<u>o a</u> supervisor immediately!
>
> **Principle 3**
>
> 2. Who asked for tha<u>t to</u> be done?
> 3. Can't you see <u>it there</u> in the account details?
> 4. This i<u>s s</u>imply unacceptable.
> 5. I though<u>t that</u> I was getting a full refund a month ago? You've alway<u>s s</u>aid that I was.
> 6. Never min<u>d that</u> now. Let me speak to a supervisor immediately!

4

5

F Intercultural matters

3 Public and private information

1

G Role-play

Specifically learners should practice:

- listening to understand the purpose of the call and the feelings of the caller ❑ **agent**
- using the zero conditional ❑ **agent and caller**
- giving instructions using imperatives and softeners ❑ **agent**
- using some common American idioms appropriately ❑ **agent and caller**
- using and understanding connected speech ❑ **agent and caller**
- using knowledge of stereotypes and cultural profiles to improve customer service ❑ **agent**
- understanding cultural differences in public and private information, and gathering private data with intercultural awareness ❑ **agent**

H Self-evaluation

Learners should evaluate themselves in particular with regard to:

- how confident they are listening to understand the purpose and details of the call and the feelings of the caller,
- using the zero conditional,
- using imperatives, softeners, and soft skills to give explanations and instructions,
- using and understanding connected speech,
- their ability to read a text and synthesize, information to answer a caller's enquiry,
- awareness of cultural norms and cultural differences,
- using intercultural awareness to ask for private information from American callers.

4 Defusing anger

A The call

The caller wants to find out why an additional $15 was added to his bill. He is frustrated that the agent cannot answer his question, and he does not want to be transferred to another department. The caller escalates the call to a supervisor, and comments that the customer service is "strange."

1 Pre-listening activity

Answer key *(suggested)*

The statement suggests that the caller is inquiring about an abnormal bill or a fraudulent credit card transaction. It also suggests the caller is frustrated at the agent's inability to explain the situation.

2 Global listening activity

Answer key *(suggested)*

This should be a low score (2 to 4). The call does not end happily; the caller is even more frustrated by the end of the call. The agent provides robotic/formulaic responses to the caller's concerns and often fails to address questions.

3 Detailed listening activity

Answer key *(suggested)*

efficient: N	distracted: N
irate: C	**robotic: A**
The caller says, "I don't like that I'm getting transferred to another call … that I might get dropped off …"	The agent says, "OK … I can only confirm with you that there was a $15 amount here …"
patient: N	**bemused: N**
Although the caller says, "I'm trying to be patient myself here," he is not actually being patient.	

friendly: N	helpful: N
While they both start off relatively friendly by sharing a joke ("You really need to know your numbers in your game"), the call quickly becomes less friendly	See notes on "Unhelpful"
rude: N	**frustrated: C**
The caller is never rude; he is merely frustrated.	The caller is clearly frustrated, saying things like, "I don't think it's right to waste time and all this inefficiency."
proactive: N	**worried: C**
	"… your customer service is strange here. Like you're not connected that much."
indifferent: A	**reactive: N**
The agent becomes more indifferent as the call goes on. At the end of the call, the agent says, "Sure. OK. Anyway, I'll be transferring your call now."	
unhelpful: A	**professional: N**
Although the caller says, "You've been really helpful," he does not mean it. The agent guesses at the solution, and does not explain it adequately. This results in the caller wanting to talk to the supervisor rather than Collections.	

B Focus on language

1 Modal verbs

1

Answer key (suggested)

obligation – *must, should, will*
>   You must finish the project by Friday.
>   You should be more careful about what you say.
>   You will do what I say.

possibility/probability – *can, could, may, might*
>   That word can be a noun or a verb.
>   He could turn up at any minute.
>   It may/might rain today.

permission – *can, could, may, would*
>   You can/may go home early.
>   Could I just make a note of that?
>   Would you just give me a minute?

logical deduction – *can't, might, could, must*
>   She can't have left the office yet.
>   He might/could be in his office.
>   They must be from the United States.

necessity – *must*
>   He must attend the meeting tomorrow.

polite offer/request – *can, could, may, shall, will, would*
>   Could/Would you repeat that, please?
>   Can/May I help you?
>   Shall we look at that again?

ability – *can, could*
>   I can read Japanese.
>   I could read when I was only four years old.

2

Answer key (suggested)

l. 2   "May I have your loan number, please?" – request

l. 5   "OK, and may I know who am I speaking with, please?" – request

l. 8   "… can I call you Kenny?" – permission

l. 12   "May I have your home address …?" – request

l. 18   "… you might have different numbers." – possibility

l. 21   "… can I just confirm …? – permission

l. 30   "And how can I help you today?" – ability

l. 33   "There shouldn't be anything extra on this bill payment." – logical deduction

l. 61   "Yes it must be something minor like that, I suppose." – logical deduction

l. 68   "And you can't answer my question?" – (lack of) ability

l. 70   "I can only confirm …" – ability

l. 80   "Yes, it must be something like that." – logical deduction

l. 89   "I might get dropped off …" – possibility

l. 93   "I wonder if I can speak to …" – possibility/permission

l. 99   "… anything else I can assist you with?" – ability

l. 113 "You should be able to give me one-stop service." – obligation

3

Answer key (suggested)

2.   He may/might be stuck in traffic.

3.   The delay could/might be because of the weather.

4.   It may/might not be plugged in.

5.   It could/might be because there is too much salt in it.

6.   She must be out of the house.

7.   There might not be enough water in the pot.

4

Answer key (suggested)

1.   It could have fallen out of my pocket. / It might have been stolen.

2.   She must have received bad news. / She might have had a quarrel with her boyfriend.

3.   She might have gotten lost on her way over. / She could have missed the bus.

4.   They must have sealed that big deal overseas. / They might have made a big profit this year.

5.   Someone must have eaten them. / Someone might have taken them.

6.   She must have worked very hard to get it. / She must have made a good impression on her boss.

7.   He might have lost it. / He can't have finished reading it.

2 Phrasal verbs (2)

1

Answer key (suggested)

1.   Separable: I'll bring the matter up with my supervisor.

2.   Separable: Can you drop the letter off on your way home?

3.   Non-separable

4. Separable: I'll look the address up on the web.
5. Non-separable
6. Separable: I'll work the exact amount out I owe you when I get home later.
7. Separable: Please put my mother up for a few days when she arrives.

C Soft skills

1 Defusing anger

1

Answer key (suggested)

The caller's frustration begins to escalate when he says:
l. 66 "… what's your name again?"
At this the point the caller wants to hold someone personally responsible for the bad service he is receiving.

Things then escalate to the point where the caller says:
l. 87 "I don't like that I'm getting transferred to another call … that I might get dropped off …"
Here the caller's focus switches from wanting an answer to the question of the $15 to wanting to complain to the supervisor about the customer service he has experienced.

2 Sounding sincere

1

Answer key (suggested)

l. 50 "I need to transfer your call to our Collections Department for them to be able to …"
Improved response: I'm afraid I'm not able to access the information I need to give you an answer to that, <u>but</u> the Collections Department <u>will</u> be able to explain it to you <u>clearly</u>. Would you like me to put you through to them right away?

l. 70 "OK … I can only confirm with you that there was a 15-dollar amount here …"
Improved response: I'm <u>sorry</u> about the <u>confusion</u> this has caused. I can <u>see</u> that you were charged $15, but I'm afraid I can't access the <u>details</u> relating to it.

l. 115 "Sure. OK. Anyway, I'll be transferring your call now."
Improved response: I'm very <u>sorry</u> about all the <u>inconvenience</u> this has caused you. I'm sure the <u>supervisor</u> will be able to <u>sort out</u> everything for you very <u>quickly</u>.

D Pronunciation

1 Understanding and using intonation to express emotions

1

Answer key (suggested)

l. 68 "Isabelle. And you can't answer my question?"
l. 75 "There! So what you are saying is … there was $15, but you're not able to explain it to me."
l. 87 "I mean I don't like that I'm getting transferred to another call … that I might get dropped off …"
l. 100 "Are you transferring me to your supervisor?"
l. 108 "And Isabelle, I mean, I'm trying to be patient myself here, you know, be courteous, all of that."

3

Answer key

1.	S	4.	A
2.	S	5.	S
3.	A	6.	A

F Intercultural matters

1 Money matters in American culture

2

> *Answer key (suggested)*
>
> | American culture information | Service skills |
> |---|---|
> | Median income levels range from approx. US$40,000 a year to around US$65,000. | A loan of more than US$10,000 is likely to be large for most Americans and will be a big decision. A good agent will understand the importance of decisions like this and will be sympathetic to repayment issues, but proactive in helping to create structured repayment pathways. |
> | Cost of a movie ticket is US$11. | A loss of a similar amount will be an annoyance rather than a catastrophe. A good agent will apologize for the trouble caused and be proactive solving the issue, but will not be overly sympathetic to the actual money amount as this would not be appropriate to the size of the loss. |
> | The average American has four credit cards. 14% of Americans carry 10+ credit cards. | This information suggests that Americans are relatively self-reliant and are able to juggle their bills and credit ratings in order to keep up with so many cards. A good agent will know when callers are knowledgeable on this subject and will adjust use of language and level of complexity to suit the competence and expectations of the caller. |
> | Americans, particularly with low and medium incomes, spend a lot of money on medical or dental bills. | Emergency requirement for medical attention or long-term treatment is likely to be a major expense that may put a lot of stress on the caller. A good agent will be sensitive to this and sympathetic to unexpected medical expenses. The agent will also be proactive in helping the caller to find a solution that will be cost-effective and will fit his/her needs. |

2 Taking responsibility and understanding blame and accountability

1

Answer key (suggested)

Strategy	Why did/didn't it work?	Improved strategy
Guessing at reasons for the US$15 deduction.	Didn't work. The agent did this because the caller wanted some kind of answer from her, and pushed several times to get this. However, she sounded very uncertain of herself, which meant that her guesses did not reassure the customer.	Agent could have said: "Typically fees of this kind relate to a one-time issue, such as an underpayment from the month before. However, because I don't have access to the reason why, I can't tell you more than that. As soon as I transfer you, you will be given the reason why the fee was deducted as well as information on whether it will happen again."
Emphasizing what she can do (e.g., "I can only confirm with you that there was a 15-dollar …" / "Before I transfer your call, uh is there anything else that I can assist you with?")	Didn't work. The agent emphasized what she was able to do. This strategy can work, but without directly taking responsibility for her inability to answer the question, it served to frustrate the caller further. The caller wanted the agent to admit that she was not able to help: "And you can't answer my question?" / "… you're not able to explain it to me."	Agent could have said: "I'm afraid I can't answer your question as to why the additional fee is there. However, I can ensure that you are put through to someone who will be able to answer that straightaway."
Paraphrasing the caller's concern at the end of the call: "That's again the 15-dollar fee, right? You don't like talking to so many people about it. Is that the problem?"	Did work. This strategy showed that the agent understood why the customer was frustrated.	This would have been better applied at the start of the call with the original concern. The agent should have paraphrased at the start to show understanding.

2

Answer key (suggested)

1. I'm very sorry to hear that. I know this must be extremely stressful and of course you will want to freeze your account as quickly as possible. Unfortunately, I'm not able to authorize this. However, I will transfer you directly to the department that can do that so we can get it done straightaway.

2. That's unfortunate. I'll officially contest this charge for you, and we'll do our best to help you get a refund from the company. However, because this company is listed as private on our systems, we cannot guarantee a refund. If we are not successful in securing a refund, you may want to consider contacting them directly.

G Role-play

Specifically learners should practice:

- listening to understand the purpose of the call and the feelings of the caller ❏ **agent**
- using modal verbs with various functions ❏ **agent and caller**
- using phrasal verbs correctly ❏ **agent and caller**
- defusing anger ❏ **agent**
- sounding sincere ❏ **agent**
- using intonation to express emotion ❏ **agent and caller**
- using knowledge of money matters in American culture and how these affect customer service ❏ **agent**
- understanding blame and accountability culture as reflected in customer expectations ❏ **agent**

H Self-evaluation

Learners should evaluate themselves in particular with regard to:

- how confident they are listening to understand the purpose and details of the call and the feelings of the caller,
- using modal verbs with their various functions,
- using phrasal verbs,
- their ability to defuse anger and sound sincere,
- using and understanding how intonation can be used to express emotions,
- their ability to read a text and synthesize information to answer a caller's enquiry,
- their knowledge of cultural norms in the USA concerning financial issues and expectations of accountability.

5 Probing for information and admitting mistakes

A The call

The caller wants to find out about what he should send in to get his camera repaired. The call progresses to the agent giving the caller advice about trying different batteries and cleaning the battery compartment before sending the camera for repair.

1 Pre-listening activity

Answer key (suggested)

This suggests that the call will be about blame and faulty products.

2 Global listening activity

Answer key (suggested)

The caller feels that his problem has been understood. At the end of the call, he says, "Sure it's straightforward what I have to do now."
The agent suggests that the caller cleans the battery compartment and tries lithium batteries before sending the camera for repair.

3 Detailed listening activity

Answer key

| 1. c | 3. a | 5. c | 7. a |
| 2. a | 4. b | 6. c | 8. d |

B Focus on language

1 The interrupted past

1

Answer key (suggested)

Because an action that was in progress (expressed by using the past continuous) is interrupted by another shorter action (expressed by using the simple past).

2

Answer key (suggested)

2. A: Where were you when the purse went missing?
    B: I was cleaning the garage when it went missing.
3. A: Why are you late for the meeting?
    B: I was driving to work and my car broke down on the way.
4. A: You promised the report by yesterday.
    B: I was just putting the finishing touches on it yesterday when I was urgently needed on another project.
5. A: How did you manage to crash the car?
    B: I was driving very carefully when a car came out of nowhere and crashed into me.
6. A: Did you burn the dinner again?
    B: Yes. I was watching a really interesting program on TV and I completely lost track of time.

3

Answer key

l. 44: "I was heading out of town in the car, and it was on the seat and it started beeping." (excuse)

l. 116: "I was using the wrong batteries and I had a similar problem." (describing past action)

l. 131: "I was using alcohol before." (describing past action)

→ **Appendix 3** (for a description of this activity refer to the Online Trainer's Manual)

2 The second conditional

1

> ### Answer key (suggested)
>
> 1. **A:** I have an awful toothache!
>   **B:** I would see a dentist if I were you. (giving advice)
> 2. **A:** Do you gamble your monthly salary on the horse races?
>   **B:** If I had enough money to spend on gambling, I would use it to pay off my debts. (improbable)
> 3. **A:** Can I drive your car into the city at top speed?
>   **B:** I think the police would stop you if you did that. (hypothetical)
> 4. **A:** Would you like to win the lottery?
>   **B:** Of course! If I won the lottery, I would buy a mansion. (improbable)
> 5. **A:** Can you do double shifts at work all next week?
>   **B:** If I had a baby-sitter to look after my son, I would be able to do double shifts. (hypothetical)
> 6. **A:** I don't want to work hard, but I want to get into the best university.
>   **B:** If I were you, I would decide which is more important because you cannot have it both ways. (giving advice)

3 American idioms (2)

1

> ### Answer key (suggested)
>
> - head out: *to leave*
>   **A:** When do you head out again?
>   **B:** I'm leaving the day after tomorrow.
> - tell somebody off: *to reprimand someone*
>   **A:** What was the problem with your boss this morning?
>   **B:** She told me off because I hadn't kept her informed.
> - What's up with it? *What is wrong with it?*
>   **A:** What's up with your car?
>   **B:** I don't know. It won't start.
> - has something to do with: *is related / connected to*
>   **A:** Does the problem have anything to do with the batteries?
>   **B:** I don't know. I'll try some other batteries and see if that solves the problem.
> - We're all set now? *Are we ready?*
>   **A:** Are we all set for the meeting?
>   **B:** Yeah, sure. We can start any time.

2

> ### Answer key (suggested)
>
> warning: *heads up*
> something that disgusts you: *turn off*
> to go to bed: *turn in*
> to celebrate someone leaving: *send off*
> to leave: *head out / head off*
> to explain: *set out*
>
> Here are some more idioms with the same verbs:
> **send**
> send packing: *send away*
> send in: *send something to an organization or authority*
> send on: *send something (e.g. a document) you have received to another person*
> send out: *send something to a lot of different people at the same time; to signal*
> send up: *make fun of someone by impersonating them*
>
> **set**
> set one back: *cost a certain amount of money*
> set straight: *clarify*
> set about: *start doing something*
> set off: *to start a journey*
> set up: *establish something like a company; prepare equipment for use*
>
> **turn**
> turn away: *refuse entrance to someone*
> turn down: *reject an offer; reduce volume/ temperature, etc.*
> turn into: *become*
> turn out: *produce something; attend; turn off (a light)*
> turn over: *give to someone else*
> turn to: *look to someone else for assistance/comfort*

C Soft skills

1 Probing questions

1

> ### Answer key (suggested)
>
> l. 14 "Can I have the first … the … return authorization number that you have?"
> l. 18 "Is your name Gary Sharpe?"
> l. 21 "OK, and phone number is 789-4763?"
> l. 26 "What charger are you using? A Rapid? Are you using a Rapid Charger?"
> l. 40 "Um you said that the camera was … has been dropped, right?"
> l. 59 "You're using a rechargeable Ultraenergy battery?"
> l. 63 "… have you tried other types of batteries, such as lithium?"

2

> ### Answer key (suggested)
>
> 1. There were enough probing questions in this call to find out in a relatively short period of time what may have caused the problem with the camera.
> 2. These questions helped the agent perform her job by identifying the potential cause of the problem efficiently, as well as recommend solutions to the caller.
> 3. These questions led to a solution that might help the caller solve the problem quickly without the need to send the camera in for repair.

3

> ### Answer key (suggested)
>
> **Scenario 1**
> In this scenario, the caller will be reluctant to admit that he/she dropped the phone several times. The key challenge in this scenario is to use probing questions effectively to find out how the phone was damaged but without making the caller feel hostile. Probing questions that could be used include:
> • So what brand and model number is this phone?
> • Would you like to keep the same color?
> • And can you tell me exactly what happened? How did the screen get damaged?

> **Scenario 2**
> In this scenario, the key challenge is to probe politely around a potentially sensitive topic. The agent should not make value judgments (implicit or explicit) about the sleeping arrangements.
> Some probing questions used could include:
> • OK, a room for two. What bed arrangement would you like? Twin? Double? Queen?
> • Your first and last name please and those of your traveling companion?
> • And the check-in date is?
> • Any special requirements? Smoking, or wheelchair-accessible? Anything like that?

2 Admitting mistakes

1

> ### Answer key (suggested)
>
> 1. I'm sorry. I meant no disrespect by it Mr. Andrews.
> 2. Oh, I apologize for that. Is "Wavchowski" how I say it?
> 3. I'm sorry about that mixup – I was looking at the wrong file. You're absolutely right. Our records show you've never made a late payment. My apologies.
> 4. Oh dear. Looks like someone made a typo when they entered the data. I'll fix it right away. OK, that's all changed now. Rest assured that no letters have been sent to the incorrect address in the past, so you haven't missed anything as a result of this mixup.

D Pronunciation

1 Silent consonants

1

> ### Answer key (suggested)
>
> l. 5: "I'm gonna sen**d** my camera in."
> l. 11: "An**d** the information, my …"
> l. 11: "I nee**d** to send in …"
> l. 17: "eigh**t** three …"
> l. 18: "jus**t** a moment …"

3

> **Answer key (suggested)**
>
> 1. The meeting ran la<u>te</u> this morning.
> 2. I haven't seen <u>h</u>im since las<u>t</u> week.
> 3. What is <u>h</u>er husban<u>d</u> doing a<u>t</u> the office? He shoul<u>d</u> be at home.
> 4. Can you hol<u>d</u> jus<u>t</u> for a moment? I won'<u>t</u> be long.
> 5. I think that <u>h</u>e woul<u>d</u> become the mos<u>t</u> valuable employee.
> 6. Could you sen<u>d</u> tha<u>t</u> documen<u>t</u> to <u>h</u>im today, please?
> 7. The hotel burne<u>d</u> down las<u>t</u> summer.
> 8. We <u>h</u>ave never spent our vacatio<u>n</u> near home.

2 Silent syllables

1

> **Answer key**
>
> | Word | Pronunciation |
> | --- | --- |
> | basically | basic'ly |
> | vegetable | veg'table |
> | worsening | wors'ning |
> | actually | actu'ly |
> | automatically | automatic'ly |
> | separate | sep'rate |
> | primary | prim'ry |

2

> **Answer key**
>
> espec'lly
> mem'ry
> batt'ries
> act'lly

F Intercultural matters

1 Higher education

2

> **Answer key (suggested)**
>
> To send two children to a college where tuition costs $20,000 a year for four-year courses with living expenses at $10,000 per year would cost $240,000. For a family with an average income of around $50,000 per year, this represents an extremely large financial commitment to make. Families often begin college funds for children as soon as they are born because saving up this amount of money takes many years.

2 Family ties

1

> **Answer key (suggested)**
>
> This fact suggests that American culture values and encourages the following:
>
> - **independence** for young people (almost half live further than 100 miles from home)
> - **family ties:** the "other" half of the learners stays closer to home. This suggests that although independence is highly valued, family ties also play a major role for significant sections of society.
> - **self-sufficiency:** related to independence. The ability to look after oneself when living far from home in order to pursue a degree.

2

Answer key (suggested)

Core values	Shared or different? (individual answers)
2. Independence	
3. Nuclear family units	
4. Saving to provide the best education for children	
5. Freedom to live together before marriage	
6. Completing high school education	

Non-Core values	Shared or different? (individual answers)
2. Marriage should not end in divorce	
3. The elderly live with their families for support	
4. Getting a job as soon as possible to support extended family	
5. Completing college degree	
6. Moving away from your hometown.	

3

Answer key (suggested)

Customer profile	Agent service skills needed
Caller has a son he wants to give the camera to. Caller's son is at college and caller does not see him much.	Since the son is probably quite far away (caller does not see him often), a good agent would understand that this camera being fixed is very important to the caller , and has an emotional impact on him as well. A good agent would be sympathetic to the problem and reassure the customer that the camera will be as good as new for his son to use.
Caller is planning to give his son a second-hand camera. The camera he has bought runs on batteries that are cheap to replace (which was why the caller said he bought it).	Since the caller is giving his son a second-hand camera that is cost-effective to maintain, we might infer that the caller is cost-conscious. Because we know that a college education is expensive, and that the caller is likely to be paying for it, this could mean that financial issues are difficult for this caller. A good agent will be sympathetic to the situation and look for cost-effective solutions (i.e., cheaper batteries) as well as highlighting solutions that are free (cleaning the camera himself / using repair services under warranty).

4

Answer key (suggested)

2. Wow – that's great. I bet she'll enjoy New York. Do you think she'd appreciate something classy that will be very stylish, but won't go out of fashion too quickly? Or would she like the latest in the fashion scene? We've got very affordable options in both cases.

3. Oh, I'm very sorry to hear that. That's very kind of you to look after her. I'm sure she really appreciates it. Just to clarify, you'll be putting your mother-in-law personally as a driver on your car insurance?

G Role-play

Specifically learners should practice:

- listening to understand the purpose of the call and the feelings of the caller ❏ **agent**
- using the second conditional to give advice ❏ **agent**
- using the interrupted past ❏ **agent and caller**
- using American idioms correctly ❏ **agent and caller**
- probing for detailed information ❏ **agent**
- admitting mistakes ❏ **agent**
- using connected speech in a natural way ❏ **agent and caller**
- understanding how cultural attitudes to higher education and family ties can impact calls ❏ **agent**

H Self-evaluation

Learners should evaluate themselves in particular with regard to:

- how confident they are listening to understand the purpose and details of the call and the feelings of the caller,
- using the second conditional and the interrupted past,
- how confident they are using idioms,
- using language and soft skills to probe for details, give advice, and admit mistakes,
- using connected speech in a natural way ("silent" letters and syllables),
- their ability to read a text and synthesize information to answer a caller's enquiry,
- their knowledge of cultural norms in the USA concerning higher education and family ties.

6 Dealing with complaints and checking information

A The call

The caller in this call wants to find out why her mobile phone is over its limit when the available minutes have not yet been used. She also wants to know why her bill was over the usual amount previously. The agent explains that the reason for both of these issues is that one of the two phones (owned by the caller and her husband) has been receiving text messages, which are charged at a premium. The agent then puts a block on this function so that the problem does not occur again.

1 Pre-listening activity

Answer key (suggested)

This suggests that something is costing the caller a lot of money. The call is likely to be a complaint, a request for a refund, or a request to change whatever is costing the caller a lot of money. However, the fact that the caller says "Just curious" suggests the caller is not upset or irate.

2 Global listening activity

Answer key (suggested)

1. *Friendly* – she laughs a lot and has a very friendly tone of voice.
2. *Not very competent with technology* – she never sends text messages.
3. *Not focused on money* – she did not complain about the penalty payments for the June bill at the time, and she did not seek a refund for the current bill.
4. *Thorough* – she has noticed the charges on the billing and explored the amount of minutes remaining on her phone.
5. *Polite* – refers to agent as "ma'am" and is very polite throughout.

3 Detailed listening activity

Answer key

1. F (They only went over the 800 minutes on *one* phone according to the agent.)
2. F (She found out the information on the phone.)
3. T
4. T
5. F (She says she and her husband don't know how to use the text function.)
6. F (They have had the phone for two *and a half* years.)
7. F ("We call each other, but we never go over the minutes.")
8. F (Text messages are blocked on *both* phones.)

B Focus on language

1 Modals used to express obligation

1

Answer key (suggested)

Caller: Yes, I'd like to complain about my new credit card access. I haven't got my pin number yet! I need my credit card!

Agent: Oh, I'm so sorry about that. <u>Do you need to</u> use your credit card today? What time do you need access? I might be able to assist you in accessing your card over the phone.

Caller: Oh, that would be fantastic. Thanks so much. I <u>must</u> pay some overdue bills or else my electricity will be shut off.

Agent: OK, well, you <u>just need to</u> give me your Social Security number.

Caller: Oh, let me see. I <u>will have to</u> try and remember it!

Agent: You <u>don't have to</u> give it to me right now, but call me back in five minutes.

Caller: <u>I'll have to</u> call my husband. He has a good memory for those kinds of things!

Agent: OK call me back in five minutes, and I <u>will need you to check some</u> other details like bank card details, phone numbers, birthdays, etc. <u>I'm supposed to</u> gather this information to be sure you are really who you say you are!	**2** Passives
Caller: OK, fair enough. I'll talk to you in a few minutes. Oh, by the way, <u>do I have to</u> wait for 12 hours after activating the card, or can I use it straight away?	1
Agent: No, you can use it immediately!	

2 Passives

1

> **Answer key (suggested)**
>
> I'm being asked to pay twice.
> I was told it would be sent to me yesterday.
> I was informed it was late.
> It needs to be sent to me immediately.
> I'm being told that my bill hasn't been paid.
> I haven't received what I was promised.

→ **Appendix 4** (for a description of this activity refer to the Online Trainer's Manual)

3 Phrasal verbs

1

> **Answer key (suggested)**
>
> | Line | Verb | Preposition | Meaning |
> |---|---|---|---|
> | l. 35 | check | out | review |
> | l. 48 | add | up | compute the total |
> | l. 61 | set | up | programmed |
> | l. 77 | come | on | please understand |
> | l. 85 | work | out | understand the process |
> | l. 101 | look | into | investigate |
> | l. 107 | gone | over | exceed the limit |
> | l. 107 | figure | out | understand |
> | l. 108 | going | on | happening |
> | l. 146 | rake | up | accumulate |

C Soft skills

1 Active listening

2

> **Answer key (suggested)**
>
> **Rule 1**
> Agent: I can imagine how frustrating that is. And I'm sorry no one contacted you earlier about this. I see here from the notes that the technician had trouble with his vehicle and it had to have urgent repairs. We'll ensure you're his first stop tomorrow morning at 9 a.m. so you won't need to take any more time off work than is absolutely necessary. Will that time suit you tomorrow?
>
> **Rule 2**
> Agent: So just to clarify. You're wondering what the $39 administrative fee is for? It is actually your annual fee for use of the credit card, but on your statement it is called an administrative fee.
>
> **Rule 3**
> Agent: I'm sorry you weren't made aware of this fee. Let me see if I can get the fee reduced since you're one of our premier customers. If you can just hold for a minute, I'll check this with my supervisor.

3

Answer key (suggested)

I can understand how that could be confusing. Let me just check I've understood this correctly. You have a plan with 800 shared minutes, and you think that you have been charged for mobile to mobile calls and night time and weekend calls, right? That shouldn't be the case, but if you wouldn't mind holding for a minute, I'll be able look into your bills to figure out the reason behind this charge.

4

Answer key (suggested)

Scenario 1

My deepest sympathies for your loss. I want you to know that there is no need to worry about the policy number. I know you are worried about having misplaced it, but I can get the policy information by entering your husband's date of birth and mailing address into the system. Are you able to provide me with that information?

Scenario 2

I'm terribly sorry for the mixup and can understand your frustration. Let me just confirm that you need to arrive in London at 1p.m. tomorrow London time. This will mean you'll need to leave NYC tonight local time. Let me just check the availability on these flights. Please be reassured we'll do our best to get you on a flight tonight at no extra cost. If you could just hold for one minute, I'll see what our options are.

D Pronunciation

1 Word stress and meaning (1)

1

Answer key

Thank you for calling <u>Fast Phones</u>. This is <u>Ally</u>. How can I <u>help</u> you today?

2

Answer key

1. The bottle is certainly empty. / The bottle is currently empty, but it was not empty at a point in the past.
2. The bottle, not another item, is empty.
3. The bottle is empty, as opposed to being full or half full.
4. This specific bottle is empty, not any other bottle.

Additional Listening

1. We do other kinds of messages but not **text** messages.
2. **We** don't text message, but somebody else might.
3. Can you open the **door** – not the window?
4. Can **you** – nobody else – open the door?

4

Answer key (suggested)

2. **Agent:** Can I have your husband's Social Security number, please?
3. **Agent:** We sent you a check for five thousand dollars.
4. **Caller:** I haven't received any notification from you guys.
5. **Caller:** You must give me a full refund.
6. **Caller:** I don't want him to have access to this card.

5

Answer key (suggested)

2. **Meaning:** I was never given a policy number.
   Emotion: The caller may be feeling frustrated at not being given a policy number.
3. **Meaning:** I have a policy, but I don't know the actual number.
   Emotion: The caller may be irritated that he/she can't solve the issue without a number.

F Intercultural matters

2 Friendly or furious?

1

2

3

Caller uses humor to build rapport	Caller uses humor to express anger	Comments on agent's response	Improved response
–	l. 52–53 "They shouldn't be billing that amount in my view."	Agent responded by saying "Oh, I'm so sorry." This correctly interpreted the laughter as expressing concern or annoyance rather than building rapport.	–
–	l. 76–77 "No, we don't even know how to do that. Come on!"	Agent responded by immediately correcting the customer, "No, incoming, ma'am."	Acknowledge the caller's frustration due to the misunderstanding. By saying "Yes, I understand that you don't send text messages at all. Actually what I'm seeing is that you have received messages …"
l. 128 "No."		Agent responds by continuing with problem-solving: "OK, the 6521 phone has also gone over 800 minutes …"	Agent should have already understood that the caller is not aware of complex phone functions (such as "roaming"). Acknowledge that the caller has already explained that she doesn't know how to text message. Say: "I know this is unlikely, but you don't by any chance know if your phone has been put on 'roaming'?" After the caller's response, say: "Yes, I see, I just had to check!"

3 Responding to humor

1

G Role-play

Specifically learners should practice:

- listening to understand the purpose of the call and the feelings of the caller ❏ **agent**
- using modal verbs to express obligation ❏ **agent and caller**
- using passives forms and phrasal verbs correctly ❏ **agent and caller**
- dealing with complaints and checking information ❏ **agent**
- stressing words in a sentence to convey certain meanings ❏ **agent and caller**
- understanding humor and sarcasm ❏ **agent and caller**

H Self-evaluation

Learners should evaluate themselves in particular with regard to:

- how confident they are listening to understand the purpose and details of the call and the feelings of the caller,
- using modal verbs to express obligation,
- using passive forms and phrasal verbs,
- their ability to be an active listener,
- using language and soft skills to help deal with complaints,
- stressing the correct words in a sentence to convey certain meanings,
- their ability to read a text and synthesize information to answer a caller's enquiry,
- understanding the difference between sarcasm and humor,
- using intercultural awareness to build rapport with customers.

7 Showing empathy

A The call

The caller wants to complain about his insurance policy being canceled despite the fact that he has authorized the company to withdraw the amount required to keep the policy active. He has had this problem before and is very frustrated by the mistakes that have been made by the company. While he is complaining, he wants the agent to know that he is not angry with him personally. The agent has difficulty explaining, but remains polite, is a good listener, and ultimately does what he can to help the caller.

1 Pre-listening activity

> **Answer key (suggested)**
>
> The caller is probably complaining about a series of mistakes. Reference to his/her lawyers might be a veiled threat about what the caller will do if matters do not improve.

2 Global listening activity

> **Answer key (suggested)**
>
> 1. Personality of the caller:
>   - polite and respectful in that he tries not to get personal. The caller calls the agent "Mr. Dell" (l. 122) and ends the call by saying, "… thank you very much and have a blessed weekend." (l. 179)
>   - organized – "I have documentation of all these errors that have been made …" (l. 156)
>
>   Emotional state of the caller:
>   - losing patience – "Every time something happens they send a termination, which sends my wife through the ceiling, and myself." (l. 94)
>   - getting angry. The caller sounds angry at various points in the call, such as when he says, "I'm willing to do that!" (l. 115) and "I don't send money or checks!" (l. 163)
>   - threatening – "I just don't want to have to go to my lawyers on all these goof ups." (l. 151)

> 2. Purpose of the call:
>   The caller has received another termination notice. He is calling to complain about how he had given instructions and authorization to the insurance company to withdraw payment from his bank automatically to maintain his policy.

3 Detailed listening activity

1

> **Answer key (suggested)**
>
> The caller felt frustrated throughout the call. He was frustrated (but stayed calm) when the call began. He gets increasingly frustrated throughout the call because the company hasn't understood that the caller is willing to let them draw the amount directly from his account (e.g., "I'm willing to do that!" (l. 115); "You automatically are supposed to withdraw the payments from the account!" (l. 119).
> He stays frustrated remembering the past problems with the company [(e.g., "Someone's goofing up there and putting me through stress!" (l. 122); "It's just a stereotypical letter!" (l. 135); "Someone is failing to do their job" (l. 164)].
> Later in the call, it is obvious that he has had enough of the company's incompetence and he mentions legal action.

2

> **Answer key (suggested)**
>
>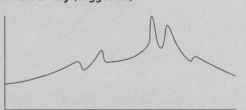
>
> First peak l. 25: "I received a termination notice."
> Second peak l. 85: "It was very clear …"
> Third peak l. 115: "I'm willing to do that! …"
> Fourth peak l. 151: "I appreciate that very much. I just don't want to have to go to my lawyers on all of these goof ups."
> Fifth peak l. 172: "… Common sense!"

B Focus on language

1 Present continuous (2)

1

> ### Answer key
>
> **Function 1:** Something happening at time of speaking.
> **Function 2:** Something in progress, but not actually happening at the time of speaking.
> **Function 3:** Future arrangements.

2

> ### Answer key
>
> 1. **Function:** something happening at time of speaking.
> 2. **Function:** future arrangement
> 3. **Function:** something in progress, but not actually happening at the time of speaking

3

> ### Answer key (suggested)
>
> l. 4: "Who am I talking to?" *Function 1*
> l. 31: "I'm just looking into this …" *Function 1*
> l. 81: "… you're still going to hear from us" *Function 2*
> l. 104: "… what we're withdrawing on your letter is uh $11,55." *Function 3*
> l. 121: "I'm not yelling at you, sir." *Function 1*
> l. 164: "Someone is failing to do their job." *Function 3*

2 Extended use of *just, actually,* and *still*

1

> ### Answer key (suggested)
>
> | Line number | Examples of *just, actually, still* | Agent uses in order to … |
> |---|---|---|
> | 31 | "I'm still here." | express that the agent was and is currently listening. |
> | 64 | "Because there is actually a letter here …" | emphasize the existence of the letter (which should reassure the customer that action has been taken). |
> | 79 | "So … I'm just going to make a request here." | express it is a simple action that the agent is about to do. |
> | 81 | "So you're still going to hear from us" | emphasize continued service. |
> | 139 | "to still keep the policy in force right now" | emphasize correcting the situation and control the customer's feelings. |
> | 165 | "OK, actually, I'm going to make just such justifications." | emphasize cooperation between agent and customer. |
> | 173 | "So we'll just have to wait for the decision." | express that nothing else can be done but wait. |

2

> ### Answer key (suggested)
>
> 1. Yes we did actually send it out yesterday. It will still be in the mail, but it should be with you tomorrow.
> 2. I'm very sorry about the mixup. I'll just fix it up now and send the confirmation by email.
> 3. No problem. The application form will actually be there this week, so you won't have long to wait.
> 4. It will just take a few hours to be processed.

3 Modals used in polite requests

1

> ### Answer key (suggested)
>
> Would you mind (not) doing …?
> Would you mind if I do …?
> Would you be so kind and …?
> Would it be okay if …?
>
> Could I possibly …?
> Can/Could you just …, please?
> Excuse me. May I …?
> I wonder if you could possibly/just …

2

> ### Answer key (suggested)
>
> l. 16: Could you please give me …
> l. 23: And how can I help you with this policy, sir?
> l. 41: Can you just …
> l. 46: What is your phone number please?
> l. 55: Would you repeat, sir?

3

> ### Answer key (suggested)
>
> 1. Sorry to bother you, but would it be all right with you if I took next Monday off?
> 2. Do you think I could borrow your camera this weekend?

4 Phrasal verbs (4)

1

> ### Answer key (suggested)
>
> | Phrasal Verb | Meaning |
> | --- | --- |
> | let down | disappoint |
> | let on | reveal |
> | let through | pass |
> | let up | stop |
>
> | | |
> | --- | --- |
> | look at | observe/watch |
> | look over | skim/read quickly |
> | look into | investigate |
> | look back (on) | reminisce |

2

> ### Answer key (examples)
>
> Tom promised to come, but he *let* us *down* at the last minute.

> If I tell you a secret, you must promise not to *let on* to anyone.
> I showed the guards my ID card and they *let* me *through*.
> The rain hasn't *let up* for a week.
> He *looked at* me with sad eyes.
> Could you just *look over* this report for me, please?
> I don't know how the mistake was made, but I'll *look into* it.
> My grandparents often *look back* on the old days when they were young.

3

> ### Answer key (suggested)
>
> l. 26 "check this out" – investigate the problem
> l. 31 "looking into this" – reviewing the issue
> l. 32 "sent a letter in" – sent a letter by mail to the company
> l. 35 "draw off" – take money out of a bank account
> l. 63 "put the policy back in force" – return the policy to its former active/valid state
> l. 122 "goofing up" – making mistakes
> l. 141 "canceled out" – lapsed/no longer valid
> l. 160 "straighten it up" – fix the problem

C Soft skills

1 Evaluating the agent

1

> ### Answer key (suggested)
>
> 1. **F** (l. 173, 177): The agent has written a report, but tells the caller that he'll "just have to wait for the decision," and regarding solving the problem: "You'll be notified through writing, or if not, someone from the department will call you."
> 2. **F** (l. 62): The caller does not understand how the Reinstatement Department will help, and the agent uses jargon such as "justifications," which does not clearly communicate what is being done.
> 3. **T** (l. 173): "Yes, sir. I understand."
> 4. **T** (l. 146, 173): "So if you wanted to do that, I'm going to make such justification"; "Yes, sir. I understand."
> 5. **F** (l. 25): Caller: "I received a termination notice." Agent: "OK. Mmm let me check this out."
> 6. **F** (l. 69): The caller had problems understanding "Reinstatement Department."

2 Building relationships

1

> ### Answer key (suggested)
>
> | Line number | Solidarity cues |
> |---|---|
> | l. 41 | Can you just, not you personally, … |
> | l. 96 | "You can understand that, I'm sure you can, you sound like a reasonable person." |
> | l. 161 | "… well, not you, Dell – but someone else there, …" |

3 Showing empathy

1

> ### Answer key (suggested)
>
> 1. Oh, that's terrible! I'm sorry that happened to you. We can cancel your credit card right away and send you a replacement. Do you know your card number?
> 2. My condolences for your loss. It must be a very difficult time for you. I know the procedure may seem complicated, but I'm here to guide you through the process. It won't take too long. Do you have the policy number with you?
> 3. Oh, wow, that must be frightening! Were you able to pull over in the break-down lane? I will alert the service truck now. What was the last exit you passed?

D Pronunciation

Differentiating vowel sounds (1)

1

> ### Answer key
>
> | /ei/ | /e/ | /ɪ/ | /i:/ |
> |---|---|---|---|
> | Dale | Dell | fill | feel |
> | payment | help | give | please |
> | termination | check | it | received |
> | date | stress | did | repeat |
> | appreciate | every | this | reasonable |
> | saying | | | mean |
> | | | | keep |
> | | | | these |

3

> ### Answer key (suggested)
>
> Emma ate eggs every Easter.
> David didn't date Debbie Deeds.
> Take Tim's textbook and teach times tables.
> She sells sea shells on the sea shore.
> Peter Piper picked a peck of pickled peppers.

F Intercultural matters

2 Dealing with customer dissatisfaction

1

> ### Answer key
>
> | Caller displeasure | Agent response | Improved response |
> |---|---|---|
> | "Somebody's got a case of incompetence." (l. 123) | "Let me see –" | Yes, I can see how this would be stressful for you, but rest assured I'm going to look into the cause of the problem and fix it so that you don't have to deal with this again. |
> | "Every time something happens they send a termination, which sends my wife through the ceiling, and myself. Causes us distress. You can understand that, I'm sure you can, you sound like a reasonable person." (l. 94) | "Uh-huh. Uh, right now –" | Yes, I can completely understand why that would be frustrating for both you and your wife. What I will do to ensure this doesn't happen again is … |

"Why didn't they draw that amount?" (l. 111)	"So, if you're willing to do that, I'm going to make a justification –"	This amount was not drawn because the department did not believe they had your authorization to do so. However, I realize you have given this, so I will be addressing this issue with the department to ensure they always draw the required amount in future.
"It doesn't say you failed to pay $1,276." (l. 138)	"Yes, sir. But to keep … to … to still keep the policy in force right now … Let me see … because the policy has canceled out …"	Yes, I can see how that would be frustrating because it was not clear to you why the policy has been canceled. I will be working with you now to make sure this issue is resolved so that your policy will not be canceled again due to this problem.

2

Answer key *(suggested)*

High importance to Americans:
- accuracy and not making mistakes
- direct answers to direct questions
- taking responsibility for mistakes

Medium importance to Americans:
- punctuality
- making small talk

G Role-play

Specifically learners should practice:

- listening to understand the purpose of the call and the feelings of the caller ❑ **agent**
- using the present continuous with *just, actually,* and *still* ❑ **agent and caller**
- using modal verbs in requests ❑ **agent and caller**
- using phrasal verbs correctly ❑ **agent and caller**
- using language and soft skills to build relationships and show empathy ❑ **agent**
- differentiating vowel sounds ❑ **agent and caller**
- understanding of litigation and compensation culture ❑ **agent**

H Self-evaluation

Learners should evaluate themselves in particular with regard to:

- how confident they are listening to understand the purpose and details of the call and the feelings of the caller,
- using the present continuous tense,
- using modal verbs to make polite requests,
- using phrasal verbs,
- their ability to be build relationships and show empathy,
- differentiating between vowel sounds,
- their ability to read a text and synthesize information to answer a caller's enquiry,
- their understanding of the culture of litigation and compensation in the USA and how this could affect call center interaction,
- their ability to respond to complaints in a culturally intelligent manner.

8 Thinking aloud and building solidarity

A The call

The caller in this call wants to access the internet. The agent guides him through the process and troubleshoots the problems he is facing with his system. The caller is familiar with computers and tries to predict some of the agent's moves. The agent is patient and clear, checking that the caller understands each step before moving on.

1 Pre-listening activity

> **Answer key (suggested)**
>
> The caller is likely to be complaining about a service that he/she can't access. The caller may be requesting a refund or may want help successfully accessing the service.

2 Global listening activity

> **Answer key (suggested)**
>
> 1. **F.** Caller is never angry. At some points during the call he is frustrated, however. By the end of the call he is relieved and grateful.
> 2. **T.** Agent takes time to guide caller through the process and does not go too fast. She makes sure he understands everything.
> 3. **T.** When the caller says: "It seems it's luck that I can do it now," it shows that the issue has been resolved, even though the caller is not confident about his own abilities.
> 4. **T.** The caller knows how to navigate his computer system and tries to predict steps when troubleshooting (although these predictions are sometimes incorrect). Agent does not need to explain very simple functions (such as how to use the mouse, etc.).
> 5. **T.** The caller laughs with the agent. At one point, the caller jokes about his own abilities, at another he mentions the agent's ability in contrast with her age. On both occasions they laugh, and the intonation used makes their exchange sound amiable and builds rapport.

3 Detailed listening activity

> **Answer key**
>
> | What is the problem? | What is the solution? |
> |---|---|
> | The caller clicks on the icon to get internet access, but it doesn't work. | 1. Make sure the caller can dial up the internet.

 2. The icon the caller is using is incorrect. The caller must rename the icon and find the correct icon to access the internet. |

B Focus on language

1 Modals of ability

1

> **Answer key (suggested)**
>
> 1. wasn't able/couldn't
> 2. could have
> 3. can
> 4. Could
> 5. could/may/might

2

> **Answer key (suggested)**
>
> l. 20 "… how **can** I help you tonight?" – ability
> l. 9 "so I **can** show your Lensolutions account" – ability
> l. 23 "I'm not **able to** get online" – ability
> l. 26 "so that you **can** get on to the internet" – ability
> l. 39 "paying for service I **can't** even get on" – ability
> l. 83 "what **may** have –" – logical deduction
> l. 115 "we **should** be in the…" – logical deduction
> l. 119 "you **should** have shown" – logical deduction
> l. 129 "We **can** bring the check mark" – ability
> l. 138 "it **should** give us the same screen" – logical deduction
> l. 141 "it's luck that I **can** do it now" - ability

2 Using the first conditional for instructions

1

> *Answer key (suggested)*
>
> 1. **Exercising to lose weight**
>   You'll notice that if you exercise regularly for a few months, you will lose weight quite rapidly. Additionally, if you eat well and exercise for extended periods each day, your weight loss will be faster and more dramatic.
>
> 2. **Studying hard to get into a college course**
>   If you want to get into a good college course, you'll have to improve your grades. If you study regularly and prepare adequately for exams, you will see an improvement, which will mean you can apply to the college course of your choice.
>
> 3. **Saving money to buy a house**
>   There are no two ways about it: if you want to buy a house, you'll have to save a lot of money. In order for you to save money, you'll have to put aside at least 20% of your salary each month. Then, when you have saved enough money, you'll be able to make a down payment and take out a mortgage.
>
> 4. **Starting work on time to complete all your tasks**
>   You'll need to start work on time if you want to complete all your tasks. If you start work late, you will be rushing to complete work by the deadline, and you might not manage it.

2

> *Answer key (suggested)*
>
> l. 27 "If we can achieve that today, I'll be happy!"
> l. 59 "And if you log on using … it'll not sign us in"
> l. 149 "So the next person will be aware of what we've discussed so far, if they access that note."

C Soft skills

1 Thinking aloud professionally

1

> *Answer key (suggested)*
>
> **Scenario 1**
>
> OK, so you are having issues with your printer. There are several things that could be the source of the problem. Let's first try to see if the cables are working properly …
>
> **Scenario 2**
>
> So you are saying that your sister has been using your card without your permission, right? OK – I'm just looking into our procedure on this … If you can tell me how long you think this has been going on, we can look at the purchases made on your electronic statement and figure out how much money she has spent. Then I'll pass you on to my supervisor, who will be sorting out where we go from there.
>
> **Scenario 3**
>
> I'm very sorry to hear that! I hope that the loss hasn't spoiled your trip too much. OK – to answer your question, let me check first, because we have different procedures for different locations, different types of equipment, and it depends on your insurance plan. Can you tell me exactly what equipment was lost, which insurance plan you are on, and where you are located?

2 Building solidarity through the pronouns *we* and *us*

1

> *Answer key*
>
> (b)

2

D Pronunciation

1 Intonation when giving instructions

2

3

5

➞ See **Appendix 5**

2 Intonation and context

1

2

3

F Intercultural matters

1 Diagnosing self-reliant customers

1

2

2 Self-empowerment culture

2

Answer key (suggested)

Caller feeling disempowered	Evaluation of agent response	Improved agent response
l. 23 "And I'm not able to get online."	Agent summarizes caller's concern by saying, "So what we're trying to accomplish is for you is to install that CD so that you can get on to the internet." Use of the pronoun *we* suggests that caller will be involved in troubleshooting. This will help him to feel more empowered.	Agent's response is good. Showing that the caller will be involved in troubleshooting can help to raise feelings of empowerment. Agent could have slightly improved the response by reassuring the customer (e.g., by using language such as "don't worry" with her responses).
l. 109 "Uh … no."	The caller sounds very frustrated when he says this, and the agent immediately responds: "Oh. No. OK, let's try this one then. "Right click the Start button." She continues to use solidarity-building pronouns and uses upbeat intonation to balance his disappointment.	This agent's response is very good. The only possible improvement would be reassuring phrases such as, "No worries, we can try something else," or "That's OK, we've got other options here …"
l. 141 "No, it seems it's luck that I can do it now. Doubl sound mighty young, and you can do it all …"	At this point the caller and agent laugh and the agent uses the reassuring phrase, "No, you're doing great."	The agent's response is good. It could have been improved by extending the light conversation with a joking remark, such as: "You should have seen me the first time I had to install the internet! You wouldn't be saying that then," or, "It's much easier having been brought up in the computer world."

G Role-play

Specifically learners should practice:

- listening to understand the purpose of the call and the feelings of the caller ❑ **agent**
- using modal verbs to express ability ❑ **agent and caller**
- using the first conditional to give instructions ❑ **agent**
- using profession thinkaloud ❑ **agent**
- building solidarity by using the pronouns *we* and *us* ❑ **agent**
- recognizing different contexts from intonation ❑ **agent and caller**
- recognizing self-reliant customers ❑ **agent**
- understanding the self-empowerment culture ❑ **agent**

H Self-evaluation

Learners should evaluate themselves in particular with regard to:

- how confident they are listening to understand the purpose and details of the call and the feelings of the caller,
- using modals of ability,
- using the first conditional to give instructions,
- their ability to use professional thinkaloud,
- building solidarity by using the pronouns *we* and *us*,
- recognizing different contexts and messages from intonation,
- their ability to read a text and synthesize information to answer a caller's enquiry,
- their knowledge of American self-empowerment culture to positively impact calls.

9 Keeping control of an aggressive call

A The call

The caller has been contacted by her insurance company and has received a letter with a check for $9.92. She does not understand why, and wants the check explained. The agent discovers that before the $9.92 check was sent, another check was sent for $842, and that the $9.92 was not included in this original sum, when it should have been. Therefore, the insurance company sent a second check for $9.92 to cover the difference. The caller did not receive the first check for $842 and suspects that someone else has cashed this check illegally.

1 Pre-listening activity

> **Answer key (suggested)**
>
> The caller is probably complaining about something that he/she thinks someone should be punished severely for. This could be an illegal action or very serious mistakes that could incur legal liability.

2 Global listening activity

> **Answer key (suggested)**
>
> | Caller | Agent |
> |---|---|
> | angry | robotic |
> | threatening | intimidated |
> | concerned | unhelpful |
> | persistent | polite |
> | aggressive | incompetent |
> | frustrated | timid |
> | upset | |

3 Detailed listening activity

> **Answer key (suggested)**
>
> 1. a) 3. b) 5. a)
> 2. c) 4. c) 6. b)

B Focus on language

1 Expressing regret

1

> **Answer key (suggested)**
>
> 2. If I hadn't driven so fast, I wouldn't have crashed into another car.
>   I should have driven more carefully. Then I wouldn't have crashed into another car.
> 3. If I hadn't left my MP3 player out when I went to the bathroom, it wouldn't have been stolen.
>   I should have taken my MP3 player with me to the bathroom. Then it wouldn't have been stolen.
> 4. If I hadn't forgotten to set my alarm clock, I wouldn't have been late for work.
>   I should have set my alarm clock. Then I wouldn't have been late for work.
> 5. If I hadn't cooked the meat badly last night, I wouldn't have been ill all night.
>   I should have cooked the meat properly last night. Then I wouldn't have been sick.

2

> **Answer key**
>
> l. 59: "I shouldn't have paid for the policy."
> l. 108: "I mean if you hadn't called me, I wouldn't have been calling you, would I?"
> l. 130: "Oh, I shouldn't have even bothered to!"
> *Should have* is used more often.

2 Making comparisons

1

> **Answer key (suggested)**
>
> 2. The next time I come here, I want better service than I have had this time.
> 3. The food at this restaurant isn't much better than that place that closed down last month.
> 4. This is the worst plane trip I have ever experienced.
> 5. That concert was a lot better than the last one I went to.
> 6. That test was the easiest I've ever had; I think I've gotten a high score.

3 Idioms and phrasal verbs

1

2

C Soft skills

1 Keeping control of an aggressive call

1

2

3

2 Sounding "robotic"

1

> ### Answer key (suggested)
>
> l. 13: "That policy number is not coming up in our system, ma'am. Are you the owner of the policy?"
>
> l. 50: "OK, because actually, ma'am, there's a lot of Robert Fowlers coming up in the system, so for me to be able to segregate it, I'll need his date of birth."
>
> l. 94: "OK, well, the most I can do is to have this one sent over for further research, because we are seeing here the check with a signature on it."
>
> l. 170: "And that's the reason why I'm putting this for further research, ma'am. I'm going to be reporting this one … that you did not receive the check. However, we've received a copy of the encashed check."

D Pronunciation

1 Word stress and meaning (2)

1

> ### Answer key (suggested)
>
> 1. **Agent:** You should make payments on or before the due date.
>   **Caller:** I have **never** missed a payment.
>   **Agent:** Oh, dear, I'm so sorry I was looking at the wrong file. I'm so sorry about that.
>
> 2. **Agent:** I don't think there is anything you can do about this.
>   **Caller:** So what do **you** plan to do about this?
>   **Agent:** I'm terribly sorry, but that program is now obsolete and we don't have tech support for it anymore. I suggest we upgrade you to an updated version.
>
> 3. **Agent:** The storm has damaged some cabling.
>   **Caller:** That's not **my** fault!
>   **Agent:** Absolutely. I didn't mean to imply that it was. The repair crews are out making the necessary repairs. The most recent update states that it will take another 24 hours.
>
> 4. **Agent:** It may take some time.
>   **Caller:** How **long** do I have to wait?
>   **Agent:** I apologize, but I don't have an exact time. However, typically processing for this takes to 3-4 business days.

2

> ### Answer key
>
> 1. **You** really should've done that.
>   Meaning: Not someone else
>
> 2. You **really** should've done that.
>   Meaning: Reinforcing the obligation.
>
> 3. You really **should've** done that.
>   Meaning: A strong obligation.
>
> 4. You really should've **done** that.
>   Meaning: This action really needed to be taken.
>
> 5. You really should've done **that.**
>   Meaning: That specific thing, not something else.

3

> ### Answer key (suggested)
>
> Student A to read aloud:
>
> 1. What **can** he do?
>   Meaning: What possibilities are available?
>   Context and/or feeling: Situation seems hopeless.
>
> 2. She **said** she is leaving.
>   Meaning: Speaker is repeating/emphasizing.
>   Context and/or feeling: Listener is not sure whether to believe it.
>
> 3. Why did you **come**?
>   Meaning: Speaker did not expect listener to be there.
>   Context and/or feeling: Could be disappointment/strong surprise in speaker's tone.
>
> Student B to read aloud:
>
> 1. I don't think **you** understand.
>   Meaning: Speaker thinks someone else could understand, but not the listener.
>   Context and/or feeling: Speaker is condescending
>
> 2. Why did he use **that**?
>   Meaning: Speaker is referring to a specific item.
>   Context and/or feeling: Speaker might be surprised or confused.
>
> 3. **Should** I read it?
>   Meaning: Speaker is unsure about whether to read it or not.
>   Context and/or feeling: Curious or inquisitive tone.

4

> **Answer key (suggested)**
>
> It **might** be better = Speaker is making a (weak) suggestion.
>
> Did you **give** it to her? = Speaker is emphasizing whether the item was given (as opposed to being lent or sold).
>
> **Can** you help him? = Speaker is unsure about the possibility of helping this person.
>
> We can't **run** there = Running is not possible, but other methods of getting there may be possible.

F Intercultural matters

1 Direct answers to direct questions

1

> **Answer key**
>
> 1. a) 2 = (too direct)
>   b) 3 = (too indirect)
>   c) 1 = appropriate
> 2. a) 2 (too indirect)
>   b) 1 = appropriate
>   c) 3 (too direct)
> 3. a) 3 (too direct)
>   b) 2 (too indirect)
>   c) 1 = appropriate

2

> **Answer key (suggested)**
>
> 1. 2c) is a rude response, as it accuses the customer very directly and would be likely to cause offense.

4

> **Answer key (suggested)**
>
> (For American culture)
>
> 1. Unfortunately my supervisor is unavailable right now, but I'll be more than happy to help with your concern, or if you prefer, my supervisor could give you a call back.
> 2. OK, I can see that there has been some confusion here. Just give me a moment to look into what happened on our end in more detail, and then I'll be able to answer all your questions and we can get to the bottom of this.

> 3. I can understand your concern. Let me assure you that we have procedures in place to prevent somebody else from cashing this check. I'll be able to help you register this problem so that we can ensure your protection.

G Role-play

Specifically learners should practice:

- listening to understand the purpose of the call and the feelings of the caller ❏ **agent**
- using the third conditional to express regret ❏ **agent**
- making comparisons ❏ **agent and caller**
- using idioms and phrasal verbs ❏ **agent and caller**
- responding to an angry caller by defusing, apologizing, and keeping control of the call ❏ **agent**
- interpreting caller attitude and emotion through word stress ❏ **agent**
- giving direct answers to direct questions ❏ **agent**
- saying *no* ❏ **agent and caller**.

H Self-evaluation

Learners should evaluate themselves in particular with regard to:

- how confident they are listening to understand the purpose and details of the call and the feelings of the caller,
- using the third conditional and *should have done* to express regret,
- making comparisons,
- using language and soft skills to respond to angry callers, apologize, and keep control of the call,
- interpreting caller attitude and emotion from word stress,
- their ability to read a text and synthesize information to answer a caller's enquiry,
- their ability to answer direct questions politely and fairly,
- their ability to say *no*.

10 Dealing with sarcasm

A The call

The caller in this call is complaining that the contact name on her company billing is incorrect. She has called many times to try to rectify this matter and is extremely frustrated at the amount of time it has taken. The agent tracks the previous agents the caller has spoken to and decides to transfer the call to the ASD (Authorized Solution Department).

1 Pre-listening activity

> **Answer key (suggested)**
>
> This suggests that the caller has lost patience with a recurring problem.

2 Global listening activity

> **Answer key (suggested)**
>
> 1. The caller is being billed under the wrong name. She has called before to get this issue resolved.
> 2. The caller is frustrated because she has had to follow up many times and still can't get a resolution. The agent feels sorry that the caller has had such a hard time getting the issue resolved. The agent also feels nervous of the caller because she is obviously annoyed.

3 Detailed listening activity

1

> **Answer key**
>
> 1. F   5. F
> 2. T   6. T
> 3. T   7. T
> 4. F   8. F

B Focus on language

1 Conditional sentence rules – and how to break them

1

> **Answer key (suggested)**
>
> Zero conditional: to express facts, habits, rules, and regulations
>
> First conditional: a real condition with a probable result, sometimes used to give instructions.
>
> Second conditional: an unreal condition with an improbable result.
>
> Third conditional: unreal past, sometimes used for expressing regret.
>
> | Conditional type | Example and meaning |
> |---|---|
> | Zero | When it rains, things get wet. |
> | First | If I work all night, I will be tired tomorrow. |
> | Second | If I used the dictionary more, I would develop better vocabulary. |
> | Third | If I had listened, I would have known not to do that. |

2

> **Answer key**
>
> | Sentence | Meaning |
> |---|---|
> | If we went to the football match in the rain, we'll get really wet. | It is unlikely that we will go to the match, but if we do, we will definitely get wet. |
> | If he goes to Tokyo next week, he'd be able to go to the conference. | It is likely he will go to Tokyo next week, so he can attend the conference. |
> | If you were going to save for that car, you would have put by at least US$10,000 by now. | If the person really intended to save for a car, he/she would have already put by $10,000, but has not done so. |

If you hadn't spent all your money, you would be able to buy a car now.	If the person hadn't spent all his/her money in the past, he/she would be able to buy a car in the present.

Answer key *(examples found in the transcript)*

l. 53 "If they were changing it, they would've done it by now."	No changes have been made, and the caller doesn't expect any changes to take place.
l. 72 "… since you would like this account to be under the name of Fitwell Construction. We can do that."	It is important for the caller to have the name changed, and the procedure is possible.

2 Modals with several functional meanings

1

Answer key *(suggested)*

l. 2: "May I have your account number please?" = request

l. 9: "May I have your full name please?" = request

l. 16: "… may I know the company name …?" = request

l. 25: "… I need to get the matter rectified …" = obligation

l. 28: "… maybe I could help you." = offer

l. 28: "How may I help you?" = offer

l. 47: "Well, it should be under my husband's name." = expectation/obligation

l. 64: "… you need to fill out this form …" = obligation

l. 69: "… this shouldn't be an issue." = expectation/obligation

l. 74: "We can do that." = ability

l. 77: "And what would that do?" = possibility

l. 80: "This will change the name …" = promise

l. 83: "… it'll take one billing cycle …" = prediction

l. 110: "Where will it end?" = prediction

l. 112: "I can understand that …" = ability

l. 121: "They can't do anything locally." = ability

l. 128: "We will forward your issue …" = promise

l. 154: "We'll have the issue resolved …" = promise

3 Active and passive forms

1

Answer key *(suggested)*

2. Yes, we sent the check. (active)
    Yes, the check has been sent. (passive)

3. You haven't paid your last bill. (active)
    The last bill hasn't been paid. (passive)

4. It's the amount you agreed to. (active)
    It's the amount that was agreed to. (passive)

4 American idioms (3)

1

Answer key *(suggested)*

1. The speaker has been a loyal customer, but is angry now and might not use this service in the future.

2. The caller doesn't care about the process as long as the end result is speaking to the supervisor.

3. The speaker feels despondent about how complicated the process has been and the fact that it doesn't appear to be heading toward a resolution.

4. The caller has been given lots of different solutions and doesn't feel confident the new one will lead to anything.

5. The local agent/store doesn't have the authority to perform the task that will resolve this issue.

6. The caller is upset that there is no consistency in the answers she gets. The statement implies that the people he/she is speaking to are being dishonest.

C Soft skills

1 Dealing with conflict

1

> ### Answer key (suggested)
>
> | Line number | Summary of conflict or disagreement | Improved agent response |
> |---|---|---|
> | l. 19 | Agent addresses the caller as "Miss." | Agent could have asked first how to address the caller. |
> | l. 20–25 | Caller is upset that she has had to call many times about this issue. | Instead of saying that it is not showing in her record, the agent could say: "Is there another business name you use?" |
> | l. 53 | Caller asks why a change of name on billing is so complicated. | Agent could have confidently reassured the customer: "We have a procedure to do that." |
> | l. 99 | Caller is upset because no one has returned her call. | Agent did well to show empathy by saying that she understands how the caller feels. Agent could have improved this response by also apologizing and proactively reassuring the customer: "I'm sorry that no one was able to get back to you. However, we can resolve this issue right now." |

2

> ### Answer key (suggested)
>
> l. 27: "Yes, I understand that, ma'am. Um maybe I could help you. How may I help you?"
>
> l. 45: "And you want it to be changed under your husband's name"
>
> l. 51: "Uh because we can actually change this …"
>
> l. 81: "You just need to fill it out and send it back to us, and it'll be one billing cycle to take effect."
>
> l. 154: "We'll have the issue resolved right away …"

2 Responding to sarcasm

1

> ### Answer key (suggested)
>
> 1. I'm sorry you've been transferred so many times. Let me reassure you that the next department will be able to resolve your issue. I'll update them on what we have talked about so far, so they can take over from here.
>
> 2. I'm sorry if I didn't express myself clearly before. Let's start over and I'll do my best to help you out.
>
> 3. I'm sorry about having to put you on hold again. If you prefer, we could organize a call back? Will you be available in ten minutes?

D Pronunciation

1 Differentiating vowel sounds (2)

1

> ### Answer key (suggested)
>
> | /uː/ | /ʊ/ | /æ/ | /ɔː/ |
> |---|---|---|---|
> | do | pull | that | sorry |
> | to | put | contact | not |
> | you | could | at | got |
> | resolution | would | ma'am | on |
> | solution | should | actually | contact |

F Intercultural matters

1 Women's independence

1

> ### Answer key for American culture
>
> 1. **T/F** (depending on the region, society, religion, etc.)
> 2. **T/F** (depending on the region, society, religion, etc.)
> 3. **F**
> 4. **T**
> 5. **T**
> 6. **T**
> 7. **T**
> 8. **T**

2

> ### Answer key (suggested)
>
> | Core values |
> |---|
> | independence |
> | ability to earn and succeed in business |
> | equality with men |
>
> | Non-core values |
> |---|
> | marriage and motherhood being the main achievements/expectations for women |
> | marriage as a requirement in order to have children |
> | stopping work for prolonged periods for pregnancy / care of children |

G Role-play

Specifically learners should practice:

- listening to understand the purpose of the call and the feelings of the caller ❑ **agent**
- using conditionals correctly ❑ **agent and caller**
- using modals for different functions ❑ **agent and caller**
- using active and passive forms ❑ **agent and caller**
- understanding and using idioms ❑ **agent and caller**
- dealing with conflict ❑ **agent**
- differentiating vowel sounds ❑ **agent and caller**
- using awareness of American values of women's independence and of multiculturalism to help bridge the culture gap ❑ **agent**

H Self-evaluation

Learners should evaluate themselves in particular with regard to:

- to understand the purpose and details of the call and the feelings of the caller,
- using conditionals,
- using modals for different functions,
- using active and passive forms,
- understanding and using idioms,
- using language and soft skills to help deal with conflict,
- differentiating vowel sounds both in production and reception,
- their ability to read a text and synthesize information to answer a caller's enquiry,
- their knowledge of American attitudes toward women's independence, multiculturalism, and the American Dream.

troubleshoot	breaking up
something is down	heads up
give it another try	pick up
get back on track	end up
down to you	take a look

Extra idioms

iron out	through the roof
had it out	turns out
by the book	pull up
cut it out	not flying
drop the ball	follow up

iron out: To solve problems/sort out issues (*We'll keep talking until we can iron out any remaining problem.*)

had it out: To openly confront someone with a problem (*I had it out with her about always getting me to cover her overtime.*)

by the book: According to the rules (*He's very efficient and expects everyone to behave by the book.*)

cut it out: To stop doing something (*I'm going to ask you to please cut it out because it's annoying me.*)

through the roof: To make someone furious (*Every time this happens I go through the roof.*)

turns out: To happen in a particular way (*It turns out that we actually received the check last week!*)

pull up: To retrieve information, typically from a computer (*Let me just pull up your account history.*)

not flying: Not working; can be used to mean "not believable" (*What you're telling me isn't flying.*)

follow up: An action after something has happened to review new developments (*I'd like to follow up the status of my order.*)

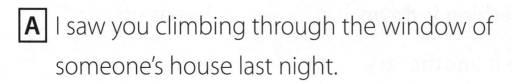

Scenarios

A I saw you climbing through the window of someone's house last night.

B I saw you leaving the movie theater with a girl/guy that wasn't your girlfriend/boyfriend.

C I saw you running down the street. I said hello but you ran right past me.

D I saw you at a nightclub, but you'd told me earlier that you were tired and didn't want to go out.

E I saw you at work last night in the boss' office. No one was there.

F I saw you last night shouting at someone on the street.

G I saw you yesterday wearing a swimsuit in the library.

H I saw you in my neighborhood last week. But you live so far from there.

I I saw you dancing on a table in a restaurant last night.

account / close	**bill / send**
tell / wait	**give / poor service**
inform / extra charges	**expect / pay**
car / damage	**do / late package**
computer / fix	**explain / problem**

PHOTOCOPIABLE

✂

Role 1

Caller:

You are calling because you cannot fix the color on your new flat screen television. Call customer support for help.

Role 1

Agent:

You need to tell a customer how to adjust the color on his/her new flat screen television.

Role 2

Caller:

You are calling customer support to complain about not being able to pay your bill online. You can't seem to make it work.

Role 2

Agent:

You will explain to a frustrated customer how to pay a bill online.

Role 3

Caller:

You need to find out how to change your account password. You have tried twice already. Call customer support for assistance.

Role 3

Agent:

You need to explain effectively to a customer how to change his/her password.